BILLY GRAHAM

Evangelistic Association

Dear Friend,

I am pleased to send you th_____ _____ *the Cross* by
Henry Blackaby, a longtime frie__ __ this ministry and a frequent
speaker at the Billy Graham Training Center. I believe its message will
help you appreciate and experience the transforming power of the cross
in a brand new way.

Many of us know the importance of the cross in providing for
our salvation, but the blessings don't end there! Freedom from sin,
victory over the enemy, and a fulfilled spiritual life are just some of the
benefits of being willing "*to take up* [*our*] *cross daily and follow* [*Christ*]"
(Luke 9:23, NIV). I pray you'll discover the joy that comes from
walking the crucified life with Him.

For 60 years the Billy Graham Evangelistic Association has
worked to take the Good News of Jesus Christ throughout the world
by every effective means available, and I'm excited about what God
will do in the years ahead.

We would appreciate knowing how our ministry has touched
your life. May God richly bless you.

Sincerely,

Franklin Graham
President

If you would like to know more about our ministry,
please contact us:

IN THE U.S.:

Billy Graham Evangelistic Association
1 Billy Graham Parkway
Charlotte, NC 28201-0001
billygraham.org
info@bgea.org
Toll-free: 1-877-247-2426

IN CANADA:

Billy Graham Evangelistic
  Association of Canada
20 Hopewell Way NE
Calgary, AB T3J 5H5
billygraham.ca
Toll-free: 1-888-393-0003

EXPERIENCING
the
CROSS

HENRY BLACKABY

This Special Edition is published by the
Billy Graham Evangelistic Association with
permission from WaterBrook Multnomah.

MULTNOMAH BOOKS

This Special Edition is published by the Billy Graham Evangelistic Association
with permission from WaterBrook Multnomah.

EXPERIENCING THE CROSS
published by Multnomah Books

©2005 by Henry T. Blackaby
ISBN: 978-1-59052-480-0

Cover design by Studiogearbox.com

Italics in Scripture quotations are the author's emphasis.
Unless otherwise indicated, Scripture quotations are from:
The Holy Bible, New King James Version
©1984 by Thomas Nelson, Inc.
Other Scripture quotations are from:
The Holy Bible, *English Standard Version* (ESV)
©2001 by Crossway Bibles, a division of Good News Publishers.
Used by permission. All rights reserved.
The Holy Bible, New International Version (NIV)
©1973, 1984 by International Bible Society,
used by permission of Zondervan Publishing House
The Holman Christian Standard Bible (HCSB)

Published in the United States by WaterBrook Multnomah, an imprint of the
Crown Publishing Group, a division of Random House Inc., New York.

MULTNOMAH and its mountain colophon are registered trademarks
of Random House Inc.

Printed in the United States of America

Library of Congress Cataloging-in-Publication Data
Blackaby, Henry T., 1935-
Experiencing the Cross / Henry T. Blackaby.
    p. cm.
ISBN 978-1-59328-289-9
Previous ISBN 1-59052-480-2
    1. Christian life—Baptist authors. 2. Holy Cross. I. Title.
BV4509.5.B545 2005
232'.4—dc22
                                        2005016999

CONTENTS

PART THREE
THE CROSS IN THE BELIEVER'S EXPERIENCE

TAKE UP YOUR CROSS AND FOLLOW

A Quest for Deeper Understanding

J esus knew that His followers had difficulty understanding—
or bearing—His clear teaching about what He faced after
their final trip to Jerusalem. Death on a Roman cross was a hard
thing to comprehend, let alone accept. Even so, He patiently
taught them what that cross would mean—to Him, to them,
and to the whole world.

He told them: "He who does not *take his cross* and follow
after Me is not worthy of Me" (Matthew 10:38). He said "to
them all": "If anyone desires to come after Me, let him deny
himself, and *take up his cross daily,* and follow Me" (Luke 9:23).

And in plain words He declared: "Whoever does not *bear his
cross* and come after Me cannot be My disciple" (Luke 14:27).

The cross is not just His; the cross is mine, and the cross is
yours. It's an unconditional and uncontestable requirement if
we would follow Him as a disciple. Would it not be important,
then, for us to clearly understand the cross's role and meaning
in our lives?

There is nothing more central to the entire Christian life

than this theme. It's an absolute essential in the experience of every believer, the very heartbeat of our faith. This is true for many reasons, and in this book I want to explore some of them. As we journey together through these pages, I want to introduce you to how the cross reveals incredible dimensions of the heart and mind of God. In fact, we cannot begin to appreciate God's eternal purposes— or His eternal nature—without a thorough understanding of the cross of Christ.

Too many of God's people are missing what He intends for them to experience, and an inadequate grasp of the cross lies at the heart of this tragedy.

Too many of God's people are going through life missing most of what their Father in heaven intends for them to experience, and an inadequate grasp of the cross lies at the heart of this tragedy.

STAYING WITH SCRIPTURE

I'm greatly honored that the Lord has granted me this opportunity to teach you, though in a sense I tremble when I consider the nature of these truths, truths that affect lives for eternity. The cross is one of the most difficult topics for me to handle, and I'm fully aware that to teach a truth wrongly or inadequately is no minor matter. It's very serious to God and has serious consequences for His people. To grasp only a partial truth is to have only a partial encounter with God, and so much is needlessly missed.

So our time together in these pages will focus on the

Scriptures and the fullness of what they tell us about the cross. As a steward of God's truth, I want to accurately divide His Word—to carefully confront each passage before God in the context of the entire Bible.

In one sense, our goal in this book is simple. We want to locate key Scriptures on this theme, carefully unfold them, and provide fuel for what I hope will be choice and productive moments for meditation and careful thought in the coming days—and for the rest of our lives.

As we apply what we encounter here—as we seek to let these truths penetrate and transform our daily lives—we will experience wonderful results from this investment of our time.

I fully recognize that the Holy Spirit alone is our teacher. He may use me as a tool, but no human teacher can open your heart and convince and convict you of the truth of God's Word and how it bears on your life. Only His Spirit can do that. And as He does, you're actually *experiencing* God; His Word is not simply principles or concepts to increase your head knowledge, but a vehicle for your *relationship* with the living God, a personal encounter that anchors His truth in the center of your being, equipping and encouraging you to live it from your heart.

So I want you to *know God* in all the Scriptures we explore together—and then apply what He shows you.

THAT YOU MAY BE OVERWHELMED

My prayer is that this book's message will be an open door to so much more—that you'll discover truths in Scripture that will challenge and encourage you for the rest of your life. I strongly encourage you to obtain this book's companion Study Guide to guide you in your quest, and to keep it open as you explore the pages to come.

In the months and years to come, may you always be captivated and compelled by the magnitude of what God has done in the cross.

PART ONE

The Cross in the Heart and Mind of God

Where It All Began

*"It has been given to you to know
the mysteries of the kingdom of heaven."*

MATTHEW 13:11

When we speak of the cross in its larger biblical meaning, we aren't thinking just of the crucifixion of Jesus—about His experience with the wood and the nails. It's a much, much bigger picture than that. In fact, we're viewing God's entire plan to redeem a world. We're looking at the whole redemptive event...as *God* sees it, not just as we perceive it.

So "the cross" isn't just the physical cross, His physical death on an actual beam of wood, though this was certainly at the critical center of God's plan and purpose. But the essence of what happened that day went far, far beyond the cruel physical realities of execution by crucifixion.

The cross transcends the physical dimension, and it also transcends time. To fully understand it, we must see the cross as the whole work of God that began in eternity, for Jesus is the "the Lamb slain *from the foundation of the world"* (Revelation 13:8), and our eternal life is something "which God, who cannot lie, *promised before time began"* (Titus 1:2). How amazing! Even before the time of Adam and Eve and their fall into sin, the cross was on the mind and heart of God.

As the cross reaches back into eternity, so it thrusts forward as well.

Just as the shadow of the cross reaches back into eternity, so it also thrusts forward. The full meaning of the cross ultimately includes the resurrection of Jesus, and later we'll see how this unbreakable link between His death and resurrection became the foundational message of the early church. And so it remains to this very day.

There's absolutely nothing in all of human history that equals this event we call the cross. But in the first part of this book, I want you to especially think of it as more than history's biggest fact; I want you to allow the Spirit of God to lay the heart of God over your own heart, so you begin to sense what the cross meant to our Father in heaven.

CHAPTER I

THE DIVINE NECESSITY OF THE CROSS

Was There No Other Way?

It is the gift of God.

EPHESIANS 2:8

When we recall the horror and frightful injustice of God's pure and blameless Son being crucified, the question often comes: *Why?* We want to know: Could there not have been some other way? Was there no other way to save us from sin?

If you haven't yet done so, I urge you to stand in the presence of God and ask Him, "Why did Jesus have to die?" Then linger in prayer until He gives you His answer.

Throughout the Scriptures, God makes clear the divine necessity of the cross. It had to happen; it was God's purpose, and *there was no other way.* If there had been, we can be absolutely certain that God would have provided it.

That's why, in this world of so many religions, a Christian declares unashamedly that Jesus Christ alone is the way and the truth and the life, and that no one can come to the Father and to eternal salvation except through Him. If the cross was God's only way of providing human redemption, then Jesus Christ is surely the only Savior there is for all mankind.

ETERNITY AS GOD VIEWS IT

The reason we often fail to grasp the divine necessity of the cross is that we don't view eternity as God views it. What does God know about eternity that you and I often fail to realize?

Recall in your mind the familiar words of John 3:16. If you could choose one word that represents the core—the very heartbeat—of what God is saying here, which word would it be? "Loved"? "Gave"? Perhaps "everlasting life"?

Actually, it's the word *perish*.

Think about that: "For God so loved the world that He gave His only begotten Son, that whoever believes in Him should not perish but have everlasting life." Death is at the very foundation of that statement—eternal death—a destiny that's inescapable by our own efforts.

In Ephesians 2:12, Paul tells us to remember something we often forget: "You were without Christ…having *no hope* and without God in the world." Humanly speaking, none of us has any eternal hope of anything…except to perish.

Yet this inescapable fact brought a response from God's heart, one that causes us to bow in wonder and awe as we truly consider it: He so *loved* the world that He *gave* His only Son… so we would *not* perish!

Something about that word *perish* made the cross eternally

necessary, requiring God to give up His Son, with no other effective strategy being possible. That word *perish* says something about eternity that we don't usually take in.

We fall short of seeing eternity as God does because we fail to view sin as He views it.

And the reason we fall short of seeing eternity as God sees it is that we fail to view sin as God views it.

THE PROOF OF SIN'S MAGNITUDE

How serious is sin?

Serious enough that to provide a way to deal with it, God the Father ordained the death of His own beloved Son, a death far more profound than physical death, as we'll study later. His Son was "holy, innocent, undefiled, separated from sinners" (Hebrews 7:26, HCSB); His Son was "a lamb without blemish and without spot" (1 Peter 1:19); "In Him was *life,* and the life was the light of men" (John 1:4). But sin—your sin and mine—necessitated this One's death.

Have you realized, therefore, how the cross reveals more of the magnitude of sin than all the wars and atrocities and human cruelties throughout recorded history?

God understands the seriousness of sin because all sin—*every* sin—is a personal offense against our God and our Creator. In that sense, there are no "little sins"; any and every sin a person commits places that person in enmity with the Father.

Not many people seriously think of themselves as God's enemy. Even believers often resist this way of thinking. They'll say with all sincerity about their past, "Well, I wasn't really going *against* God; I just wasn't going with Him." But they're sincerely wrong. God's perspective is all that matters, and He says in His Word that we were His enemies (Colossians 1:21). Or as Jesus put it, "He who is not with Me is against Me" (Matthew 12:30).

FOR THE SAKE OF HIS GREAT NAME

In Ezekiel 36, God is ready to announce to His people the new covenant which will initiate our spiritual rebirth and renewal. Speaking through the prophet, the Lord will tell the people of God, "I will cleanse you from all your filthiness and from all your idols." He will promise them, "I will give you a new heart and put a new spirit within you…. I will put My Spirit within you and cause you to walk in My statutes" (Ezekiel 36:25–27).

But first He tells His people something else. He lets them know that what He's about to do, He is doing not for their sake, "but *for My holy name's sake*, which you have profaned among the nations wherever you went. And I will sanctify My great name, which has been profaned among the nations" (vv. 22–23).

And how did God sanctify His great name among the people of Israel? He sent them into captivity in Babylon and destroyed Jerusalem and the temple. He did this to restore the holiness of His name, because His people in their sin had profaned His name among the nations. God severely chastened His covenant people in full view of the nations. All the nations could see what God did to His chosen ones, and all could see and begin to understand that the God of Israel is a holy God.

That's how serious Israel's sin was in God's eyes.

Ezekiel 36 is a passage God has powerfully used in my own

heart and life, and I'm often disturbed by all that it implies. When Christians today sin consistently, they affect how the world understands God. In fact, they profane His name by their sin. What then should we expect God to do? Doesn't the world today need to see and know that God is holy? Wouldn't God be entirely right and just, therefore, to bring severe affliction upon His people today, so the nations of the world can see His holiness displayed through His discipline of His chosen ones?

Wouldn't God be entirely just to bring affliction upon His people today so the world can see His holiness displayed?

Don't take this passage lightly. It devastates me to think about it, and causes me to pray, "O God, is there anything in my life, in word or deed, that misrepresents You to people who watch or listen, causing them to take lightly who You are? Are they kept from hearing You because of how I live or what I say? If that's so, I ask You, Lord, to do in me what's necessary to cause them to realize that *You take sin seriously.*"

God's Radical Treatment of Sin

God knows full well—as we could never know—the appalling destructiveness of sin. He *knows* what sin has done to us; He *knows* how it hurts and impairs us. For every sin we've committed, He understands the full harm done to ourselves and to others, as well as the awful affront which it is to Him. In the cross, therefore, He made complete and total provision for every aspect of what sin has done or ever could do.

And as we'll see later, because of the totality of what God did in the cross, absolutely nothing can now come into our lives to make us less than what God wants us to be and to become. In Christ and in the cross, God has already abundantly provided us with everything we need to deal with everything that confronts us.

This is true because God, through the death of His Son, purposed to deal *radically* with sin—not just with our individual sins (plural), but with the sin nature in human beings, with the whole presence of sin (singular), which is the root cause of all our individual sins.

REMINDERS ALL AROUND US OF SIN'S SERIOUSNESS

Failing to view sin seriously shows how little we understand about the reality that surrounds us every day of our lives. God has given us reminders of the seriousness of sin in the form of His judgments against sin in Genesis 3, judgments that continue to this day.

As a pastor for a church in Saskatchewan on the prairies in the heart of Canada, I officiated at many funerals. When those funerals occurred in the depths of winter, the graves had to be dug in ground that was frozen several feet down, hard as a rock. It made me think of the judgment the Lord God pronounced upon Adam: "Cursed is the ground because of you" (Genesis 3:17, ESV). Ever since Adam's sin, God has cursed the ground so that it's unyielding, or stays prone to yield the wrong things—"thorns and thistles" (v. 18), and requires painful toil to produce our food. If we take notice of this and think about it, we may wonder why God continues to bring such a judgment. Don't you suppose it's meant to serve as a constant reminder of how serious sin is to the mind and heart of God?

Or think of His judgment upon Eve and on every mother since then: "In pain you shall bring forth children" (v. 16). When a mother today experiences the intensity of labor pains, do we say, "Thank You, Lord God, for reminding us of the reality of the seriousness of sin"?

In the graciousness of God, every moment of experiencing His continuing judgment provides us an opportunity to remember how tragic sin is, how it turns us into His enemies, and how costly it is for God to deal with it.

Every moment of experiencing God's judgment provides an opportunity to remember how tragic sin is.

That's why it's incredibly good news that "when we were enemies we were reconciled to God through the death of His Son" (Romans 5:10). Our sin against God, our enmity against Him, required nothing less than the cross; and that ultimate sacrifice is exactly what God provided!

JESUS RECOGNIZED THIS DIVINE NECESSITY

Jesus Himself knew and accepted this divine necessity of the cross. This is clear in His first mention of the cross in the Gospels, in Matthew 16:21:

> From that time Jesus began to show to His disciples that He must go to Jerusalem, and suffer many things…and be killed, and be raised the third day.

The Savior didn't hint that these things *might* happen, or even predict that they *would* happen—but rather declared that they *must* happen. There could be, there would be, no other way.

Jesus again emphasized this necessity in the very significant teaching moments He had with His disciples after His death and resurrection:

> He said to them, "O foolish ones, and slow of heart to believe all that the prophets have spoken! *Was it not necessary* that the Christ should suffer these things and enter into his glory?" (Luke 24:25–26, ESV)

To demonstrate this necessity to them, He went directly to Scripture, to the Old Testament:

> He said to them, "These are the words which I spoke to you while I was still with you, that all things *must be fulfilled* which were written in the Law of Moses and the Prophets and the Psalms concerning Me." And He opened their understanding, that they might comprehend the Scriptures. Then He said to them, "Thus it is written, and *thus it was necessary* for the Christ to suffer and to rise from the dead the third day." (Luke 24:44–46)

He was telling them, "All this *had* to take place—the Scriptures themselves say so." Thus was it written, and thus was it necessary.

Paul taught the same thing: "Christ died for our sins *according to the Scriptures*" (1 Corinthians 15:3). The cross was inevitable—planned by the Father from the beginning, and plainly revealed to His people in His Word.

So whenever you come into God's presence and ask Him, "Why did Jesus have to die? Was there no other way?"—let Him show you from the Scriptures how the cross was necessary for the redemption of the whole world. Then let Him apply that truth to your heart. Let it sink in how it was all *for you...* and exactly what you need.

STRAIGHT FROM THE FATHER'S HEART

How God Views the Death of His Son

God demonstrates His own love toward us,
in that while we were still sinners,
Christ died for us.

ROMANS 5:8

Because it was Jesus Christ, God the Son, whose body was nailed to the cross, we sometimes overlook the activity of God the Father in our salvation. But the whole plan and purpose and implementation of our deliverance from sin is the work of the Father, coming straight from His heart.

The New Testament brings this to our attention. "All things are of God," Paul tells us, "who has reconciled us to Himself through Jesus Christ...*God was in Christ* reconciling the world to Himself" (2 Corinthians 5:18–19). *In* Christ and in the cross, God Himself was achieving our reconciliation.

This is why we read in John 3:16, "For *God* so loved the

22

world that *He* gave His only begotten Son…" From beginning to end in the plan of redemption, God was linked in union with His Son, and in that union, He—God the Father—was actively redeeming a world to Himself.

THE ACTIVITY OF THE FATHER

For this reason, when you try to understand the cross and the love of God, when you seek to value and appreciate some of the dimensions of all that was in His mind and heart, you have to consider how much He absorbed *into Himself* to bring forgiveness for our sin. We can only imagine the burden upon the Father as His spotless Son went to the cross to have the sin of the world placed upon Him. God was "in Christ reconciling us" even when our Savior cried out from the cross, "My God, My God, why have You forsaken Me?" Even this was the plan and purpose and activity of God, carried out through the obedience of His Son.

The entire work of bringing back a lost world was the effort of the Father.

So the entire work of bringing a lost world back to God was the effort of the Father, who chose to do it through His Son. It was the movement of the Father from beginning to end that won our salvation.

Always in Scripture, it's the Father who purposes and plans and initiates. He works through the Son to accomplish His work, then the Spirit takes what the Father has purposed and brings it into reality in the life of His people.

So it was the Father in His love who purposed our salvation

and put together everything about our redemption, and it was the Son through whom the Father accomplished it. And because of what Christ accomplished, you're now born again by the Spirit of God, who takes everything God gave His Son and makes it real to you, just as Jesus promised about the Spirit: "He will glorify Me, for He will take of what is Mine and declare it to you" (John 16:14). The Spirit, God's precious gift and our Counselor and Friend, implements in your life what the Son completed on the cross according to the Father's eternal plan and intention. And all of this flows from the Father's heart.

THE SUFFERING SERVANT FORETOLD

The prophet Isaiah gives us an intimate and powerful prophecy of the suffering Servant who bears our sin and sorrow (Isaiah 52:13–53:12), revealing the Father's heart in an extraordinary way. Written hundreds of years before the crucifixion of Christ, it details His humiliation and anguish. Much of this passage is probably familiar to you, but I want you to see it afresh from the perspective of the heart of God.

The very first words in this prophecy signal for us the active role of the Father and the yielding of the Son to the Father's plan and purpose. The Lord God says, *"Behold My Servant…"* (52:13). The Father is announcing to us here, "I want you to see One who is obediently serving Me in all that I'm about to show you."

And what does this passage show us? What do we learn about this Servant?

We see that the Father plans for His Servant to endure

intense rejection and physical suffering:

> He is despised and rejected by men....
> He was despised, and we did not esteem Him.
> He was wounded... bruised....
> He was oppressed and He was afflicted....
> He was led as a lamb to the slaughter....
> He was cut off from the land of the living....
> He was stricken.... (53:3–8)

Hundreds of years before that day in Jerusalem when the Messiah was beaten and scourged, Isaiah recorded in this Scripture how His face would be so disfigured that He would hardly be recognizable—"His appearance was so marred, beyond human semblance" (52:14, ESV).

Let me ask you: What do you think was on the heart of God, knowing that His only Son would become a man so that He could take away the sin of the world, suffering such cruelty and indignity and shame in the process?

Can you imagine how God had to restrain all of heaven? The entire angelic host would doubtless at many moments want to intervene, as they shouted, "This is our Lord! This is the King of kings! This is the Lord of heaven! We cannot let these men do this to Him!"

The twelve legions of angels Jesus spoke about in the Garden of Gethsemane must have been waiting on tiptoe, ready to respond to the first hint of a summons from their Lord. The Father would have to hold them back and declare, "This is part of what I've deliberately purposed from the beginning.

I want those who come to know My love to understand it as thoroughly and completely as they possibly can, and the quality of love I want to see in them depends on *how much they know.*" For this reason, our heavenly Father lets us see these things in Scripture, so we can know and understand.

When I read passages like Isaiah 53 and try to meditate and think about the cross from the Father's heart, there are times when I have to say, "Father, there's no way I could imagine the full meaning of these words. But I'm going to ask if somehow, in Your grace and in Your mercy, You'll kindly bring me to an increasing measure of understanding of what You mean in these verses." If you ask Him to do that as you take time alone with Him—He'll do it. And in response, your love relationship with Him will deepen beyond what you have ever experienced. You will sense the Father's heart in new and surprising ways.

As we view the sacrifice of Christ unfolded so profoundly in the book of Isaiah centuries before it happened, the Father is telling us, "You need to understand: *I knew all this ahead of time; I felt it all ahead of time,* knowing the whole weight of your sin would be focused on my Son. I want you to know My heart, and to understand that all of this was there when I purposed to bring you salvation."

OUR SIN AND THE SIN-BEARER

There's no doubt in Isaiah 53 about *why* the Servant must be treated so cruelly and suffer so horribly.

It's sin.

Our sin. Yours, and mine, and the sins of us all: "All we like sheep have gone astray; We have turned, every one, to his own way" (53:6). Every one of us is afflicted and diseased by sin and selfishness—therefore it's "*our* griefs" that the Servant bears; it's "*our* sorrows" that He carries; it's for "*our* transgressions" that He was wounded, and it's for "*our* iniquities" that He was bruised and crushed (53:4–5). Because of the loving purpose of God, this suffering is what creates the opportunity and occasion for you and for me to be forgiven.

The final lines in Isaiah 53 contain the whole of the gospel of the cross in response to our sin:

> He poured out His soul unto death, and He was numbered with the transgressors, and He bore the sin of many, and made intercession for the transgressors. (53:12)

Do you begin to see the magnitude of the love of God? When you read John 3:16, it sounds so simple: "God so loved the world that He gave His only Son." Then you read Isaiah 53—and you see that familiar gospel verse through a fresh set of eyes.

IT PLEASED THE FATHER

The most astounding verse in this chapter is one that for a long time I couldn't think about without weeping:

> It pleased the LORD to bruise Him [or "crush Him," as other translations render it]; He [God the Father] has put Him [His Servant] to grief. (53:10)

It *pleased* the LORD? Yes. This crushing of His Son was actually God's willing, deliberate action, entirely approved and acceptable to Him—and all for you and me.

In the next line, as Isaiah keeps the suffering Savior in view, he acknowledges to the Lord God, "You make His soul an offering for sin." God the Father deliberately caused *the soul of His Son* to be an offering for our sin.

Can you see the eternal heart of God—and be amazed by it?

There's something in the infinite heart of God that can accept and ordain the cross. What the death of His Son would accomplish somehow outweighed the pain of bringing this about. The intended outcome, the effect, the result—this was behind all that God purposed in the suffering of His obedient, sacrificial Servant.

> *There's something in the infinite heart of God that can accept and ordain the cross.*

And what was that outcome?

We see it touched on many times in this passage, first in 52:15: "So shall He sprinkle many nations." This is the sprinkling of blood we see so many times in the Old Testament in regard to sacrificial offerings. But this time, the offering was no animal. This time, the sacrifice was God's own beloved, anointed Servant. The blood is *His* blood, the life blood of Jesus, sprinkled not on an altar or on the mercy seat of the temple's inner sanctuary, but upon the nations of the world. In this verse, God foretells the spread of the gospel and its acceptance all around the world.

Instead of the condemnation that we all deserve for our sins, the Servant's suffering brings us "peace"; instead of the inescapable corruption of our sinfulness, "we are healed" by the Servant's lashings (53:5).

Most importantly, the Messiah's suffering will not be in vain. God promises that His Servant "shall see the labor of His soul, and be satisfied. By His knowledge My righteous Servant shall justify many, for He shall bear their iniquities" (53:11). The obedient Servant will succeed in satisfying the demands of God for dealing radically with sin.

And the glory will be His—"Therefore I will divide Him a portion with the great, and He shall divide the spoil with the strong, because He poured out His soul unto death" (53:12).

CHAPTER 3

A PROMISE GIVEN IN BLOOD

Our Sin Cost Him Everything

It is the blood that makes atonement for the soul.

LEVITICUS 17:11

Without...blood," the book of Hebrews tells us, "there is no remission" (9:22). The blood of Christ, then, is critically important in God's entire plan of redemption. Sin cannot be dealt with apart from an outpouring of blood. The Father does not forgive sin in any other way.

Simply asking God to forgive you is not what brings pardon for your sin. Nor is repentance, no matter how sincere. We can cry out to the Lord with great anguish and streaming tears, but all the sorrow in the world can never bring forgiveness if we leave out the magnitude of what God had to do to *be able* to forgive us—yielding His Son to a bloody and absolute death.

Scripture declares that "the life of the flesh is in the blood" (Leviticus 17:11), and that "the blood is the life"

(Deuteronomy 12:23). When Christ shed His blood, then, He poured out His very life to cover our sins, making a way for you and me to be made right with God.

Blood is required because when God declares the wages of sin is *death*, He means exactly that. What is it that gives us deliverance from this death that we earn because of our sin? Only the lifeblood of the Son of God.

That's how the cross makes a difference in your life. Apart from the shed blood of Jesus, all of us would face an eternity in hell, without hope, without recourse, and forever banished from the presence of God. And why is this? Because there is nothing else in all the universe, in all of time, that can cleanse us from sin.

FORETOLD AND PICTURED FROM
THE BEGINNING

From the very beginning, God began to indicate His purpose of pouring out His Son's blood for His people's salvation. Even in the Garden of Eden, when the serpent was judged for leading Adam and Eve into sin, God foretold how Satan would bruise the heel of the Son of God. It was a foreshadowing of the divine necessity of the cross.

Of course, God could have said at this time that He wouldn't allow Satan to have anything more to do with mankind or with Himself. But He didn't. Instead, it was as if He told the devil, "What you have created in the sin of Adam and Eve is going to touch My Son." There was a divine necessity at work.

Through centuries of Old Testament history, God

continued to foreshadow this sacrifice, giving His people all manner of images and activities to remind them of sin's seriousness and of the blood required for redemption.

The sacrificial system was preparing God people for the ultimate sacrifice of His Son.

The whole sacrificial system in the Old Testament was especially important in preparing God's people for the ultimate sacrifice of God's Son. These endless bloody sacrifices immersed them daily and yearly in the awareness that sin is fatal—and that without the shedding of blood, there's no remission of sins. It also pointed toward the ultimate way in which God would deal radically with sin, so His people could be forever released from sin's captivity and eternally united with God.

All these reminders helped the people of God to orient their minds and hearts to Him, so that when they came to worship they were conscious of their sin and of their need for forgiveness and cleansing to enter into relationship with God and to appreciate the greatness of His mighty salvation.

THE PASSOVER BLOOD

One of the most meaningful and symbolic events in the Old Testament is the Passover—that moment, as you remember, when the Death Angel passed over all of God's people and spared them, while slaying the firstborn son in all the families of the Egyptians. This was the final plague on Egypt, the last of God's judgments upon them, and the moment that ultimately forced Pharaoh to release the children of Israel.

Before it happened, the Lord told every Hebrew family to slay a lamb at sunset—a lamb "without blemish" (Exodus 12:5). They were to take its blood and apply it all around the doorway of their house. God told them, "Now the blood shall be a sign for you on the houses where you are. And *when I see the blood, I will pass over you;* and the plague shall not be on you to destroy you when I strike the land of Egypt" (Exodus 12:13).

God's people obeyed these commands, so that in His mercy and grace the Lord accomplished a miraculous deliverance for them, in a way marked out by blood. God was showing in a highly dramatic way that deliverance comes only with the shedding of blood.

The Lord at that time also commanded His people in the future to slay a Passover lamb each year and hold a feast of remembrance, "that you may remember the day in which you came out of the land of Egypt all the days of your life" (Deuteronomy 16:3). They were to do this continually as they lived in the promised land God was giving them—"there you shall sacrifice the Passover at twilight, at the going down of the sun, at the time you came out of Egypt" (v. 6).

This repeated sacrifice of the Passover lamb is what the people in Jesus' day would easily recall when John the Baptist saw Jesus approaching and shouted out, "Behold! The Lamb of God who takes away the sin of the world!" (John 1:29).

It was during one of these Passover celebrations in Jerusalem that Jesus was arrested and suffered and died. This was deeply symbolic, as Christ laid down His life for the people of God, even though at the time they didn't recognize it. But Jesus did recognize it, as He told His disciples in His last meal with them before His death:

> He said to them, "With fervent desire I have desired
> to eat this Passover with you before I suffer; for I say
> to you, I will no longer eat of it until it is fulfilled in
> the kingdom of God." Then He took the cup, and
> gave thanks, and said, "Take this and divide it among
> yourselves; for I say to you, I will not drink of the fruit
> of the vine until the kingdom of God comes." And He
> took bread, gave thanks and broke it, and gave it to
> them, saying, "This is My body which is given for you;
> do this in remembrance of Me." (Luke 22:15–19)

The death of Jesus Christ was what every previous Passover
had always pointed to, and what the slaying of every lamb had
foretold. But this time, God Himself was providing the Lamb,
and that Lamb was His own Son. His blood would forever
cover the life of all who believe in Him, so that their own lives
would be passed over by death.

OUR PERMANENT MEMORIAL

Besides being an Old Testament picture of the cross, the
Passover served as the permanent memorial to the Lord that
God had mandated for His people.

Has the Lord given His people today such a permanent
memorial?

He has. We call it communion, or the Lord's Supper: "For
as often as you eat this bread and drink this cup, you proclaim

the Lord's death till He comes" (1 Corinthians 11:26). It's our everlasting memorial until Jesus returns, helping us remember thoroughly and completely the shed blood and the broken body of our Lord as God's provision for us—so we never forget *what* God did and *why*.

When I served as a pastor, one of the most significant and sacred moments for me was when I guided the church in the Lord's Supper. I never tacked it on to anything else; it always became the entire service.

The death of Jesus Christ was what every Passover had always pointed to.

When Jesus instituted the Lord's Supper, it wasn't a public worship service, and He didn't open it up to everyone who'd ever followed Him. On the contrary, it was an exceedingly restricted occasion. It was only for those whom the Father had given Him, who had made an obvious commitment to follow Him to the end, and who He had carefully taught and instructed. They had a bond to Christ as Lord as well as a bond with each other.

So I came to view the Lord's Supper as His special time of encouragement for His deeply committed followers, and especially for those who've been paying a price to follow Him.

With this focus on the Lord's Supper turning our thoughts to Christ, let's move on now to study more closely all that the cross meant to the Son of God.

PART TWO

The Cross in the Life of the Lord Jesus

When Everything Hung in the Balance

The Son of Man indeed goes just as it is written of Him.

MARK 14:21

I n Isaiah 53, the Messiah and Servant of God is called "a Man of sorrows and acquainted with grief" (53:3). We see that more than ever when Jesus walked into Gethsemane and told His disciples, "My soul is exceedingly sorrowful, even to death" (Matthew 26:38).

I believe He meant this literally.

In the struggle He was entering upon, I believe our Savior came right on the edge of death, which is why His Father would send an angel to strengthen Him—to give Him just a little more time.

Let's think about that moment in Gethsemane from the Father's perspective. All that God had purposed and determined beforehand for mankind was now hanging in the balance. All that He had foretold and signified through the sacrifices and the law and the prophets, through godly men like Moses and David and so many others, all that He had demonstrated over so many centuries—all of it led up to this one moment.

In the earthly ministry of His Son, the time for teaching and for the working of miracles had come to an end; what remained in the Savior's work was that which was the most necessary and the most difficult: the cross. This is what confronted Jesus as He went to His Father in prayer in Gethsemane.

He pleaded, "Abba, Father, all things are possible for You. Take this cup away from Me" (Mark 14:36). But the Father had to answer, "I can't. I can't take it away. My eternal purpose was for this very moment."

And at that point, everything in the Father's eternal purpose for mankind's redemption depended upon whether the Savior would say, "Not My will, but Thine be done."

CHAPTER 4

HIS PATH OF OBEDIENCE

The Long Shadow of Our Savior's Cross

I do not seek My own will but the will of the Father who sent Me.

JOHN 5:30

Maybe you've wondered, as I have, what the Savior might have been praying that day.

It's a prayer session that Luke's Gospel tells us about, just prior to a quite momentous encounter Jesus had with the Twelve.

Jesus "was alone praying," Luke tells us, when His disciples approached Him. Immediately their Master had a question for them: "Who do the crowds say that I am?" After hearing the various answers, He quickly asked the more important question: "But who do *you* say that I am?"

It was Simon Peter who answered, and answered well: "The Christ of God."

Hearing this confession, Jesus for the first time spoke of

the cross to His disciples: "The Son of Man must suffer many things, and be rejected by the elders and chief priests and scribes, and be killed, and be raised the third day" (Luke 9:18–22).

With this in mind, what might we guess that Jesus had been praying about earlier, just before this solemn exchange?

The Father's Activity Revealed

In that prior conversation with His Father, I think Jesus might have been hearing something like this: "Son, each time You did a miracle, I was working in the hearts of Your disciples to tell them You are the Christ. I have been working in their hearts in everything You have said to them and taught them. I've brought these men to the point where they know You are the Christ, the Son of the living God. So now, Son, it's time. Your moment has come to begin speaking to them the message of the cross."

From that moment on, the Savior began revealing to them the essential fact of the cross.

And if Jesus, in His prayer, had then asked, "Father, how will I be sure that they know?" then the Father may well have answered, "They're approaching You now; ask them."

Looking up, Jesus saw the Twelve coming, and He spoke the critical question to them. The answer He received confirmed the faith and understanding that was in their hearts. It was the mark of the Father's activity within them. From that moment on, the Savior began revealing to them the essential fact of the cross.

In Matthew's account of this incident, we learn that

immediately after Peter confessed Jesus as "the Christ, the Son of the living God," Jesus responded, "Blessed are you, Simon Bar-Jonah, for flesh and blood has not revealed this to you, but *My Father who is in heaven*" (Matthew 16:16–17). Jesus knew that it was the *Father's* activity—then as now—that brings His followers to the fullest understanding and deepest relationship to Christ.

THE DIFFICULT PATH OF OBEDIENCE

As Jesus and His men drew near Jerusalem for the last time, Jesus continued to teach His disciples about the cross that loomed just ahead. All the while, the Savior proceeded in step-by-step conformity to the Father's will, as revealed to Him in Scripture and in times of prayer with His Father. Jesus learned what was on the Father's heart, then implemented it, living it out in flesh-and-blood reality, though His path to obedience was not an easy one.

I've had people say to me, "Henry, I find it so difficult to obey."

Sometimes I will answer, "Would you like to learn how to obey the way Jesus learned?"

"Oh, yes, I would."

Then I'll read them this verse: "Though He was a Son, yet He learned obedience *by the things which He suffered*" (Hebrews 5:8). It was in the endurance of affliction that Jesus took hold of obedience.

The previous verse in that Hebrews passage tells us how Jesus "offered up prayers and supplications, with vehement cries and tears to Him who was able to save Him from death, and was heard because of His godly fear" (5:7). Other versions read "because of His reverence" (HCSB, ESV) or "because of His reverent submission" (NIV). Jesus called out to His Father with strong crying and tears, and I think that description applies not just to Gethsemane and the cross, but also to the inclination of the Savior's heart throughout His life.

The Father heard His Son's intense cries and answered them by pointing Him to suffering and the cross—to which Jesus willingly yielded, in reverent submission, so that "He learned obedience by the things which He suffered" (5:8). Jesus allowed His suffering to keep moving Him forward on the pathway of conformity to the Father's will; He let obedience be the direct result of all His suffering.

Looking further, what then was the direct result of that obedience?

The passage in Hebrews goes on to tell us: "And having been perfected, He *became the author of eternal salvation* to all who obey Him" (5:9). Jesus in His obedient manhood was made perfect—made complete in everything God required in the Savior. As a result, He became the perfect provision God was looking for, the spotless Lamb of God who takes away the sin of the world by His sacrificial death.

No Personal Rights

To yield this way in suffering obedience to the Father's will meant that Jesus had to totally give up His personal rights. Paul tells us how Jesus "did not count equality with God a thing to be grasped, but *made himself nothing*, taking the form of a servant" (Philippians 2:6–7, ESV). As God's willing servant and the servant of mankind, Jesus "humbled Himself and became obedient to the point of death, even the death of the cross" (2:8). Jesus gave Himself over to God, to learn and do His Father's will.

One of the great hindrances for Christians is the way so many of us try to cling to our rights and what we think we deserve. The truth is, when you became a Christian, you give over all the rights of your life to the One who has the

Living by the cross of Christ means no more rights.

unquestionable right to be your Lord. You believe Him, trust Him, and let Him accomplish His purpose through your life without regard to whatever you think you might deserve. Taking up your cross—living by the cross of Christ—means no more rights.

Jesus Christ was God and equal with the Father, but He didn't cling to His rights to function as God; instead He released His life completely into the Father's hands, to let the Father work out into every corner of His life the greatness of the salvation He had planned from eternity to bring about.

And that yieldedness, that release of Himself to God, required that Jesus endure a horror that you and I—because of *His* obedience—will never have to face. This terror that He endured is something we must now explore carefully to better understand the cross.

CHAPTER 5

TRUE DEATH

A Deep and Awful Darkness Descends

*And being in agony, He prayed more earnestly.
Then His sweat became like great drops of
blood falling down to the ground.*

LUKE 22:44

As a student of history, I've been astounded to read of how many believers died for their faith in Jesus Christ. These martyrs seemed almost to welcome death, and would often devote their dying breaths to singing. Those who were burned at the stake would even taunt the flames. Death held no fear for them.

But we see our Savior in Gethsemane crying out, "O My Father, if it is possible, let this cup pass from Me" (Matthew 26:39). He was not talking about physical death; He was facing something else, something far more profound and overwhelming than anything the martyrs ever faced. Gathering over the soul of our Savior, deepest darkness and a midnight of desolation was about to descend. And it was precisely because

He faced death in these deepest dimensions that the martyrs were certain they themselves would never have to. Someone else had faced eternal death, so that they never would. Only by knowing this could they confront physical death with songs and shouts of victory.

HOMELESS HORROR

As we've observed, when Jesus entered Gethsemane, "He began to be sorrowful and deeply distressed," and He told His disciples, "My soul is exceedingly sorrowful, even to death" (Matthew 26:37–38). It appears that our Lord, in this garden, began to actually experience the first wave of suffering and sorrow that would soon engulf Him. In that moment, a sense of utter desolation washed over Him—a sense of homelessness, I believe, more intense than anything we can conceive of.

The horror of homeless anguish began to sweep over his soul.

Earlier that same evening He had spoken about His Father's home with joy. He told His disciples, "In My Father's house are many mansions," and so He encouraged them, "Let not your heart be troubled" (John 14:1–2).

Later that evening He had assured them, "I have kept My Father's commandments and *abide in His love*" (John 15:10). The Father and His love were His constant dwelling place; His Father's presence had always been the Savior's secure and loving home.

But in Gethsemane, Jesus is troubled beyond imagining as the horror of homeless anguish began to sweep over His soul.

No term strong enough can be given to such an encounter except the word *death*. Already Jesus was beginning to experience the extinguishing of His light and life as payment for the sin of the world. The inevitable casting into outer darkness that God had warned in Scripture would happen to all who do not believe, a darkness utterly void of life and light—this is what was descending upon the soul of our Savior. An outer darkness where there is weeping and wailing and gnashing of teeth—this was the pathway our Savior walked. He passed that way in our place, so that you and I need never walk that way ourselves.

And it was all utterly real. This was the essence of death... and it lies at the very heart of the gospel.

OF FIRST IMPORTANCE

We have a tendency to rely on quick, slick definitions for the distinctive words we find in Scripture. If I were to ask you, "What is the *gospel?*" you would likely answer, "Good News." And you would be right, but your answer would be extremely limited, because the gospel is far more than that. The gospel is a huge announcement of the greatness of God's salvation.

In the fifteenth chapter of Paul's first letter to the Corinthians, every word seems to be charged with that incomparably mighty salvation. Paul was making clear to the Corinthians what he'd already preached to them as being "of first importance" (1 Corinthians 15:3, NASB). He was summarizing for them the number one truth of the gospel, the heartbeat of our whole relationship to God. And here it is: "that Christ died for our sins according to the Scriptures, and that

He was buried, and that He rose again the third day according to the Scriptures" (15:3–4).

Christ died for our sins. As we hear that phrase, a key question surfaces: What does it mean to *die?*

Resorting again to a quick definition, most of us would answer something like this: "It simply means that one's body ceases to live." We think of death primarily in terms of the physical, the biological. But in the death of Christ there's a different and much deeper dimension.

DEATH'S DEEPER DIMENSION

When Jesus spoke only of physical death, He used the term "sleep" to describe it. You'll remember, for example, His words about the synagogue ruler's daughter, as He came to where her lifeless body lay in a house filled with weeping and mourning. He told the grieving crowd, "The child is not dead, but *sleeping*" (Mark 5:39). In their minds, however, there was no doubt whatsoever that she had died.

Or recall when Jesus told His disciples, on another occasion, "Our friend Lazarus *sleeps*" (John 11:11). At that point, the man had been in the tomb four days, wrapped in a shroud!

When physical life ceased, Jesus called that "sleep." When we think deeply about that, suddenly we enter a whole new understanding. We sense how there are really two kinds of death, as we employ that term. Bodily death, the ending of physical life, is only a secondary meaning of the word. True death, ultimate death, is a far more significant experience, with much more appalling and unspeakably awful dimensions.

In comparison to that dread state of being, physical death is only "sleep."

This deeper death is the death Jesus died, and according to His own promise it's also the kind of death He has saved you and me *from:* "Most assuredly, I say to you, if anyone keeps My word he shall never see death" (John 8:51). A little later He told Martha, the sister of Lazarus, "Whoever lives and believes in Me shall never die" (11:26).

> *This deeper death is the death Jesus died—and the death He saved us from.*

Never die!

And yet, when I was twenty-six, my family gathered around my father's body for a funeral service, then took that body out to a cemetery where it was buried. My father had certainly been a faithful believer in the Lord Jesus and a keeper of His Word. Why were we burying this good and well-loved man, when the Savior said that such people "shall never die"?

In truth, there's no question in my mind. Though my father's body lies in a grave at this very moment, he did not experience death. My dad *slept,* but did not die. What Jesus did on the cross made it possible for my father and all of us to escape the experience that Jesus Himself endured for our sakes. He went through the true and deepest *death*—so you and I would never have to.

Unlike the synagogue ruler's daughter, and unlike Lazarus, and unlike my father, Jesus did not just fall asleep; He actually *died*—in the most absolute way possible. And it was your sin and mine that gave to His death that deepest, darkest dimension.

CHAPTER 6

CHRIST MADE SIN

What God Did to Jesus — for Us

The death that He died, He died to sin once for all.

ROMANS 6:10

J esus was entering fully that blackest midnight of the soul when He cried out on the cross, "My God, My God, why have You forsaken Me?" (Matthew 27:46). That's the death He died for every man, the horror of an indescribable abandonment, an agonizing, consuming loneliness.

And it was *all because of sin.* In fact Paul, in 2 Corinthians 5:21, says that Christ actually *became* sin for us. What a thought!

Language fails us here. Our minds grope to understand that which finite minds can never understand. As I have placed my heart and mind into the Scriptures, seeking to better comprehend the death of Christ for our sins, I've been staggered by the immensity and enormity of this truth.

> For He made Him who knew no sin to be sin for us, that we might become the righteousness of God in

Him. (2 Corinthians 5:21)

"He"—God the Father—"made Him who knew no sin"—Jesus Christ—"to be sin for us." God made Him *to be sin.*

And please note this: In Paul's original language, those words "to be" are not there. Our English translations include them because the translators felt that such an addition helps us better understand Paul's intended meaning. In this case, however, I think the addition may take away too much. Paul stated simply that Christ was *made sin* by the Father's action on our behalf. Jesus—the One who knew no sin, the One who had *never* sinned—was *made the essence of sin* for us, all by the deliberate action and purpose of God the Father.

Notice also that this verse begins with the word *for.* Paul is declaring this truth about Jesus—that He was made sin by the Father—as a reason for something, and we see what this is in the previous verse:

Now then, we are ambassadors for Christ, as though God were pleading through us: we implore you on Christ's behalf, be reconciled to God. (2 Corinthians 5:20)

Do you see the connection Paul makes? Why do we, as ambassadors for the Savior, implore others to be reconciled to God through Christ? Because Jesus was *made sin* on their behalf by the action of the Father, that in Christ they might become the righteousness of God.

That's why we plead with people to bring their lives into

a right relationship with God. Because Christ was made sin by the active work of the Father, we have our one and only possibility and opportunity for righteousness.

THE AWFULNESS OF SIN AND ITS RESULT

When the apostle Paul, then, declares, "For the wages of *sin* is *death*" (Romans 6:23), he isn't speaking about a mere sensation of heartbeats or a flat brainwave. Instead, he refers to an eternal, utter darkness of separation and abandonment brought about by sin.

When Paul said "Christ *died* for the ungodly," (Romans 5:6), he didn't just mean that Jesus stopped breathing. No, that word *died* meant that Jesus walked straight into the terrible night of rejection and eternal separation resulting from sin, an abandonment and homelessness so complete that there's no place you can call home.

He walked straight into the terrible night of rejection and eternal separation.

Doesn't that say something about the awfulness of sin, that it necessitates such a horrible result?

Take the worst-case scenario—take every picture of judgment given in the Scriptures, every word and image given by God to try and help us realize what happens to sinners who never enter into a relationship with Christ—take it all, and we still fall light years short of the full reality Christ experienced.

All of it fell on the Savior.

He endured *all* of it—praise His name!—so you and I

wouldn't have to go through it.

The glory of the gospel—the good news—is that through the Savior's dying, the sinner lives. The wages of sin is indeed death, "but the gift of God is eternal life in Christ Jesus our Lord" (Romans 6:23). Those who will put their faith in the Son of God will never experience that pathway of utter darkness, because Jesus took the long journey for us. He took upon Himself that full-death, deepest-death, that should have been ours.

God is always thorough—and His dealings with sin reflect a thoroughness that only He is capable of. Everything our sin required—all the condemnation, all the penalty, all the *death* we deserved—fell not on us but on Jesus. Upon the Savior, upon His beloved Son, God placed "the sin *of the world*" (John 1:29). Whom does that include? All people throughout all time, from the days of Genesis, down through the centuries of human history, and continuing into all the future of human existence on earth, however short or long that may be. God laid this upon His Son "that the world through Him might be saved" (John 3:17).

Therefore Jesus now says to each of us, "Because of *your* sin and the sin of the world, I experienced in My soul the fullness of death—total abandonment and full desolation. Into My sinless and holy life, into My very being, I took your sin and the sin of the world. All of it was placed on Me. I gave up My life—so *you* could take and keep it, if you'll place your total faith and trust and commitment in what I've accomplished for you."

How Then Could We Continue in Sin?

What an awesome response this calls for from our heart. Remember the old gospel song—"Jesus paid it *all*, all to Him I owe"? Jesus indeed paid it *all*, and therefore I owe Him everything.

This is why our whole identity with Christ is found in the cross. It was there that God dealt totally and radically with sin. And it's there that God intends for us to be so united with Christ in His death that we will forever *hate* sin, *abhor* sin, and *forsake* sin. In our intimate relationship with Christ in His crucifixion, God intends for us to see sin as He does, and to *feel the horrors of sin as Christ did*—and to therefore let the Father crucify sin in our lives just as He crucified His own Son. He wants us to literally die to sin, never again to know it as a way of life—"knowing this, that our old man was crucified with Him, that the body of sin might be done away with, that we should no longer be slaves of sin" (Romans 6:6).

Our whole identity with Christ is found in the cross.

When we fully realize that our sin caused the Savior's death—death in its deepest dimension—how could anyone continue in willful sin? How can we be indifferent to sin in any form in our lives?

People today don't want to talk about sin, and often those who seem to discuss it least are God's people. Somehow we've forgotten what sin cost our Savior. But when we truly consider that utter desolation of soul and spirit, that blackness of homelessness that came over our Savior because of our sin, it creates within us an intensity *against* sin. And when this intensity burns in our heart, the result is personal holiness. It is a holiness empowered by the full message of the cross—which from the beginning has always included the resurrection. Let's turn to that part of it now.

CHAPTER 7

THE CROSS AND THE RESURRECTION

Trusting in God's Full Promise

My Father loves Me, because I lay down My life
that I may take it again. No one takes it from Me,
but I lay it down of Myself. I have power to lay it down,
and I have power to take it again.

JOHN 10:17–18

A man under arrest—that's how Jesus, the Son of God, left the garden of Gethsemane. He was on His way to be falsely accused, falsely tried, falsely convicted, and wrongly executed.

Yet He did not resist.

The Gospels tell us that while He was being tried, He remained strangely quiet. The wicked and wily King Herod "questioned Him with many words, but He answered him nothing" (Luke 23:9). Dragging the Savior before Pontius Pilate, the elders and chief priests heaped invective on Jesus and told lie after lie. Yet "He answered nothing. Then Pilate said to Him, 'Do You not hear how many things they testify against You?' But He answered him not one word, so that the governor marveled greatly" (Matthew 27:12–14).

This silence, this refusal to speak up in His own just defense, was something Isaiah had long before prophesied about God's Servant: "He was oppressed and He was afflicted, yet *He opened not His mouth*. He was led as a lamb to the slaughter, and as a sheep before its shearers is silent, so *He opened not His mouth*" (Isaiah 53:7).

WHY WAS HE SILENT?

Most of us, when falsely accused, would try to vindicate our innocence, but Jesus did not. Why do you suppose He responded this way? Why would He keep quiet?

Is your integrity before God the single most important factor in governing your behavior?

We find the answer when we see this moment from God's perspective. Jesus sought approval from One and One only: His Father in heaven. And He knew that before God, He was absolutely innocent. So why bother discussing or defending it with men? Why waste words? Why play their game? As long as God knows—that's enough.

Is that true with your life? Is your integrity "before God" and your relationship with God the single most important factor in governing your words and responses and behavior? If that is so, then it really doesn't matter what others say or do.

You don't have to react, because you stand in the confidence and peace of God Himself.

I believe that Jesus stayed silent because of the strength of His intimate, personal, confident relationship with the Father. Jesus knew that everything He was going through was the Father's will, because He'd seen it throughout the Old Testament. When His accusers demanded that He answer their charges, I'm sure He was thinking about Isaiah 53... *"He opened not His mouth."* It would only stand to reason, because Jesus lived out all His life in fulfillment of Scripture. Knowing the Scripture, He always knew how He needed to act.

Shouldn't that be true with you and me as well? As long as we know the Scripture, we don't have to be slaves to our emotional reactions when we confront difficult situations or difficult people; we can respond instead as God's Word tells us to. But if you don't know the Scripture, you'll act just like the world acts; you'll simply do what you're used to always doing in the flesh.

Jesus grasped fully the message and the promise of Scripture. And because He trusted His Father and remained yielded and obedient to His will, He knew that death—even deepest death—would not be the end of the story. The horror and anguish would be followed by the glory of His promised resurrection and the final accomplishment of God's plan and purpose for mankind's redemption. He "endured the cross," we're told in Hebrews, *"for the joy that was set before Him"* (Hebrews 12:2). As God's chosen Servant, He knew His future would be just as Isaiah prophesied: "He shall see the labor of His soul, and be satisfied" (Isaiah 53:11).

This is what gave Him hope. And it also has something to say to you and me about why we count the cost, take up our cross, and follow the Savior.

The cross isn't the end. It's the means to the end.

Our victory *follows* the cross, victory through God's resurrection power. And just around the corner, beyond the three-score-and-ten of this brief life on earth, an eternity of joy awaits.

THE NECESSARY CONCLUSION

God always connects the cross with the resurrection. This is true in His plan and purpose, and must be true in our own thinking as well, because there's no victory over sin without the resurrection. If there was no resurrection, it would mean the cross had defeated the purposes of God—the enemy would have won, and there would be no salvation.

On the cross, Jesus Christ in His body carried the weight of the sin of the world; but not until three days later, when He rose bodily from the dead, was God's plan of salvation made complete. The resurrection confirmed it: The sacrifice had been accepted! Sin had been dealt with decisively, and the unsurpassable evidence of that fact was the risen, living body of the Lord Jesus.

God always connects the cross with the resurrection.

The resurrection was the culmination and final fulfillment of God's redemptive purpose. That's why the major thrust of the apostles' preaching in the book of Acts, right from the beginning in those thrilling early days of the church, was not the crucifixion of Christ but His resurrection. This was the main theme of Peter's message to the crowds in Jerusalem on the day of Pentecost—"This Jesus God has raised up," Peter declared, "of which we are all witnesses" (Acts 2:32).

The resurrection, then, is the absolutely necessary conclusion to the whole cross event. The cross was not the end, but a necessary means to the end.

It is God's final word…not death, but *life*.

WORTHY IS THE LAMB

In His earlier ministry and teaching to His disciples, Jesus continually linked the resurrection with the cross. With equal clarity, looking ahead, He clearly saw them both on His path of obedience to God's will.

Both were very much in His conscious awareness all along. The apostle John tells us that early in His ministry, when the leaders in Jerusalem protested His first cleansing of the Temple, Jesus replied to them, "Destroy this temple, and in three days I will raise it up." John goes on to explain, "He was speaking of the temple of His body. Therefore, when He had risen from the dead, His disciples remembered that He had said this to them; and they believed the Scripture and the word which Jesus had said" (John 2:19–22).

From His understanding of the Scriptures, and from His knowledge of the Father's heart, Jesus knew that the cross *had to take place*. But He was equally aware of the divine necessity of His resurrection: "Thus it is written, and thus it was necessary for the Christ to suffer and to rise from the dead the third day" (Luke 24:46).

He knew His death was a "must."

But so was rising from the dead.

And so was His ascension into glory—the glory that we get a glimpse of in Revelation 5, where the heavenly hosts sing, "Worthy is the Lamb who was slain to receive power and riches and wisdom, and strength and honor and glory and blessing!" (Revelation 5:12).

That's what all of heaven will sing throughout eternity: *Worthy is the Lamb who was slain!* We'll gladly worship the Savior with these words, never forgetting that the Lamb whom God provided as the sacrifice for our sins was His own beloved Son. We'll spend eternity remembering it in worship before His very presence, all to His eternal praise and glory.

PART THREE

The Cross in the Believer's Experience

Where Everything Changes

I do not set aside the grace of God.

GALATIANS 2:21

One of the best of the old gospel hymns opens with these lines:

Years I spent in vanity and pride,
caring not my Lord was crucified,
knowing not it was for me He died
at Calvary.

Perhaps you can identify with spending too much of your life in vanity and pride. *Vanity* simply means that whatever you do ends in emptiness; there's nothing there. And *pride* won't let you admit it.

But though all this can be true about us, God marshals the resources of heaven to pursue us and rescue us. It's all grace; it's nothing we deserve. Simply because He loved us, He begins to draw us to Himself. Suddenly, the lights come on and the truth dawns. We experience great grief over how we've treated Him, how we never really cared that He was crucified.

Inevitably every Christian comes to stand at what the hymn called Calvary, a name for the place where the cross of Christ stood. There, as you let God open your understanding, you see the truth: "It was for *me* He died!" By faith we accept that this was God's plan, God's purpose. This was God's way of providing salvation for us.

It changes everything. Your heart receives and *knows* what before you knew only in your head. And it begins to affect the whole of your life.

"If anyone is in Christ," Paul says, "he is a new creation; old things have passed away; behold, all things have become new" (2 Corinthians 5:17). *In Christ*—that's Paul's favorite term, and we've seen it in a number of Scriptures we've looked at already. To be "in Christ" means to be in union with Him, a union that guarantees eternal life for us, just as the apostle tells us: "God has given us eternal life, and this life is in His Son. He who has the Son has life" (1 John 5:11–12).

This is what the cross accomplishes. This is what the transaction of being born again is all about. This is what happens when you genuinely ask Jesus into your heart. Being "in Christ," Paul says, means having *all* things become *new*. Everything is transformed. You're a *new* creation.

This change is huge; no transformation can possibly be greater. You go from being condemned to being forgiven. You go from irremovable guilt to being declared righteous by God—not because of your own righteousness, but because you've opened your life to receive Christ and *His* righteousness. And when God looks at you—wonder of wonders—He no longer sees your sin but the righteousness of His own Son.

If then you've been born again, if you've been redeemed and delivered through that transaction by faith, isn't it reasonable to expect that everyone around you would be able to see the evidence of it? Simply by watching your life, shouldn't the world be able to see the reality of what God accomplished in the cross?

Are you believing all that He says about the cross and responding to all that He is in His grace and love, as demonstrated in the cross? If not, you're in danger of making the death of Christ a mockery.

Be assured that the death of His Son was not a mockery to God—it was His supreme and solitary provision of salvation, fully adequate for every person everywhere in the world, at all times, under all conditions, and totally effectual to bring any and every sinner into a vibrant relationship with Himself.

We all have difficulty sometimes in remembering the difference between experiencing a true relationship with the God of our salvation and experiencing merely the practice of religion. We can practice everything correctly, do all the

"spiritual" things people expect us to do, but never progress in the relationship. But Scripture, if we approach it honestly and let it be our guide, is always pressing us up against that relationship, the close, intimate walk with God that is so essential for true transformation.

So the question I keep trying to get believers to ask themselves is this: *Where is the evidence that my life has been transformed?*

We've looked already at the cross in the mind of God and at the cross in the life of the Lord Jesus. Now it's time to turn our careful attention to the cross in your life and in mine.

CHAPTER 8

CRUCIFIED WITH CHRIST

Our Personal Experience of the Cross

*Do you not know that as many of us as were baptized
into Christ Jesus were baptized into His death?*

ROMANS 6:3

The cross is more than a doctrine; it's an *experience*.
To understand this from Scripture, I want to look
with you at some verses you're probably quite familiar with.
Unfortunately, our casual quoting of them can become so
common that they lose their meaning for us. We need to look
at them and think about them much more carefully as we
consider the reality of the cross in the Christian's life.

TOTAL IDENTIFICATION WITH THE SAVIOR'S DEATH

How real was the cross to the apostle Paul?

Certainly the most familiar passage on this would be his

statement in Galatians 2:20—"I have been crucified with Christ." How have you understood that phrase?

I think the average Christian assumes Paul is saying something like "Christ died for me." I've heard theologians discuss whether this isn't merely a "positional" statement, whether it was only "as if" Paul had been crucified with the Lord Jesus. But as a pastor, having walked alongside so many broken people who have looked to the cross for redemption and restoration, I have to conclude that no, this statement from Paul is absolutely real.

The cross isn't a doctrine to be discussed, but a fact to be experienced.

The cross isn't a doctrine to be discussed, but a fact to be experienced.

Think about what Paul actually expressed here: *I have been crucified with Christ.* He didn't state that someone had been crucified in his place; Paul said *he* had been crucified *with* Christ.

This is where all human language fails, and I don't begin to fully understand what God did with Paul. But I believe that somehow, in some inexplicable way, God let Paul understand the depths of what our sin had done to the Savior. I sense that somehow Paul's mind and heart and soul were expanded, and he was *with* his Lord at Calvary. The Spirit of God took him through a total identification with the Savior's death on his behalf.

Paul went through it personally.

And at every turn in the process, as Paul watched His dying Savior, he would cry out, "My Lord! This is where *I* should be!"

"Yes, I know," the Lord would say to him. "But, Paul, you

cannot pay this price; only I can. And I cannot avoid it, or else you will never live. You'll have no life, Paul, unless I shed My blood for you."

Paul never got over this experience. It brought a radical transformation in his life—the only response worthy of One who has paid such a price.

EXPERIENCE NECESSARY

I have been crucified with Christ, Paul said. How does that statement apply to you and me?

Again, the average Christian would think, "Well, it doesn't really."

I disagree.

If you saw Mel Gibson's film *The Passion of the Christ,* did you sense that you were being crucified *with* Christ, or that He was being crucified *for* you? I'm sure most of those who watched it had great sympathy with Jesus, but I doubt many of us sensed that we were up there on that cross, crucified and bleeding with Him. Yet I believe you and I are also called to begin understanding those depths just as Paul did, and to know the transformation that Paul knew as well.

It's helpful for us to link Paul's statement in Galatians 2:20 with something else he wrote: "For the love of Christ compels us, because we judge thus: that if One died for all, *then all died"* (2 Corinthians 5:14). The wages of sin is death, and our penalty of death had to be paid. And Jesus paid it; He died that death for all.

For this reason, *you* have died, and *I* have died. You were present on the cross; you were present in Christ. For if He died for all, then all died.

Don't just think of these things as abstract doctrines or generic symbols. *Take them into your heart and soul.* As Jesus said on another occasion, such words "are spirit and are life" (John 6:63, NASB).

There must be some point in your life where you can say— not just doctrinally, but experientially—"I have been crucified with Christ." Only the living Lord Himself can bring you to that place.

The deepest meaning of the cross and its transforming power can only be understood experientially. Don't ever equate knowing a doctrine with having experienced the reality of the truth. *The cross must be experienced to be understood.*

MAKING SELFISHNESS IMPOSSIBLE

Immediately after Paul says, "If One died for all, then all died," he adds these words: "He died for all, that those who live *should live no longer for themselves, but for Him* who died for them and rose again" (2 Corinthians 5:14–15).

Do you see the connection?

If He died for all, then we who died with Him must never again live for ourselves. If we truly understand the cross, if we ever go through the process of being crucified with Him, then it's impossible that we should simply go on living the same as before. We live no longer for ourselves, but *for Him.*

Getting a mental grip on these truths is crucial. But a mental grip won't change your life. You and I need to actually *experience* this phenomenon of being crucified with Jesus.

The cross in the Christian's life does something radical. The more you know and understand what God was doing for you—and what the alternative was if He hadn't—the more impossible it is to live your life unto yourself. It's a spiritual impossibility. Once you understand the cross, a selfish, self-centered life is simply no longer an option.

CHAPTER 9

THE CROSS BRINGS FULLNESS OF LIFE

A New Creation That Stays New

Because I live, you will live also.

JOHN 14:19

I f you could somehow go back in time and actually observe the life of the apostle Paul, would you be able to tell from what he said and how he acted that the cross was the centerpiece for his entire life?

The answer, I'm sure, is yes.

And that same yes should hold for you and me as well.

THE LIVING PRESENCE OF THE LIVING CHRIST

After affirming that he had been crucified with Christ, Paul immediately added these words:

It is no longer I who live, but Christ lives in me; and the life which I now live in the flesh I live by faith in the Son of God, who loved me and gave Himself for me. (Galatians 2:20)

Paul was making clear the result of the cross: *I myself live by the living presence of the living Christ—who now dwells within me and lives out His life through me.* Paul knew that the experience of being crucified with Christ was completely linked to the experience of being indwelt and empowered and controlled by the risen and living Christ. Paul understood that the cross is followed by the resurrection.

And he refused to settle for anything less!

Let all that God accomplished in the cross have full effect in your life.

What he declares next in this passage is this: "I do not set aside the grace of God; for if righteousness comes through the law, then Christ died in vain" (2:21). Paul refused to overlook or ignore all that God had done for him in the cross. He knew that *real* life meant Christ living out His life within him. Paul would never try to live on his own, in his own strength or by his own legalistic righteousness, because that would mean "Christ died in vain."

That last phrase in this verse is a crucial one for us all. If you don't want the cross to be emptied of its meaning and power in your life, if you want to be everything God intends you to be because of the cross, then let all that God accomplished in the cross have full effect in your life. Don't set aside what God has done and try to live apart from full dependence on the living Christ.

When Paul stated in 2 Corinthians that anyone in Christ is a "new creation," with all things becoming new in their lives, the newness he referred to was the living presence of Christ Himself. That's what's new (and *stays* new) in our lives when we live by the cross.

You now have Christ living out the newness of His life in you. He's not only cleansing you from sin, guarding you from sin, and giving you victory over sin, but He's also filling you with *life*. Don't let anybody ever tell you that the life of holiness is drab, boring, and lifeless. It is not. How could it be? It's full of the complete, abundant, overflowing life of God. It is full of joy. It is full of victory. It is full of promise and hope. As you follow the way of the cross, you'll see things you've never seen and hear things you've never heard.

CRUCIFIED TO THE WORLD

This full picture of the life-giving cross totally shaped the rest of Paul's life and ministry as he lived it out in the real world. Listen carefully to his words in Galatians 6:14:

> God forbid that I should boast except in the cross of our Lord Jesus Christ, by whom the world has been crucified to me, and I to the world.

What a powerful statement! It begins with "God forbid"—

and whenever we see Paul using that expression, we know he's making a very thorough and emphatic statement. Here he's saying, "My prayer is that God would surround me in such a way that nothing will interfere with my commitment to living by the cross."

Paul wanted the exclusive credit for his life to belong only to the cross of Christ. Because of that cross, Paul's relationship to the world around him was one of being "crucified." He knew that the world's attractions were only a mirage; nothing the world claims to offer is real. This world and its ways held no appeal for Paul because he was crucified to it. He could see more than the world sees, and what he saw was the glory of the cross of Jesus Christ and the eternal life and hope it brings.

You and I can read Paul's words here and respond in one of two ways. We can either find ourselves thinking, *Me, too, Lord,* and then moving on to something else—or by going to God and asking, "Help me to understand what this really meant for Paul and what it can mean for me."

KNOWING CHRIST JESUS AND HIM CRUCIFIED

Paul knew that the cross of Christ was the only hope for the world of his day. This was the inescapable conclusion from the message he preached everywhere he went.

In his natural self, Paul had always been a brilliant man with a strong sense of personal discipline and high moral standards. But when he came to Corinth—one of the most immoral cities in the Roman Empire—it wasn't his brilliant wisdom or his discipline or moral principles that he proclaimed. His message instead was the power of the cross. He said he came to "preach Christ crucified...Christ the power of God and the wisdom of God" (1 Corinthians 1:23–24). He confessed to the Corinthians that Christ Himself had sent him "to preach the gospel, not with wisdom of words, *lest the cross of Christ should be made of no effect*" (1:17).

> *Paul could see the power in the cross that others failed to see.*

Paul could see the power in the cross that others failed to see: "For the message of the cross is foolishness to those who are perishing, but to us who are being saved it is the power of God" (1:18). This *power,* found only in the cross, was what he wanted the Corinthians to fully embrace and experience, just as Paul had.

"When I came to you," he told them, "I determined not to *know* anything among you *except Jesus Christ and Him crucified*" (2:1–2). Paul wasn't talking about a doctrine. This wasn't simply course content for a seminary class, but a real, vital, life experience. It was this and this alone that allowed Paul to preach with power from the Spirit of God, with the result that the Corinthians' faith "should not be in the wisdom of men but in the power of God" (2:5).

Paul wanted to see the impact of the crucified Christ in every area of life for the Corinthians.

EXAMINING YOUR LIFE

It's also what God wants to see in you. If you meditate on these

Scriptures, He will thread the truth of them through your heart, then out from your heart into the rest of your life.

Take time to ask God to open your mind and heart to the reality of what Paul kept talking about: I have been crucified with Christ... Christ lives in me... I boast only in the cross of Christ... I know only Christ and Him crucified...the message of the cross is the power of God.

You and I must ask ourselves some crucial questions: How is the cross affecting *my* life? Is my life centered on the cross? Is that the reality—not just in my "theology," but in my experience? Am I experiencing the life of the living Lord? Or... does the world still have priority in shaping how I spend my time, energy, thoughts, and all that I have? Am I in any way quenching and resisting His activity in my life, setting aside the grace of God, so that the cross of Christ is made of no effect in me?

May God so work in your heart that toward all these dangers you come to respond genuinely as Paul did: "God forbid!"

CHAPTER 10

SOURCE OF EVERY BLESSING

What the Cross Releases

For all things are yours....
And you are Christ's, and Christ is God's.

1 CORINTHIANS 3:21–23

As we continue moving more deeply into the truths of the cross and their meaning for our everyday lives, one of the most staggering discoveries for our heart and soul is that the cross has procured for us unimaginable riches and blessings from God the Father.

We've seen how the full event of the cross was eternally purposed in the mind and heart of God—that it was something He ordained even before the world began. Along with this eternally-planned cross has come an incredible vastness of spiritual blessing for us in every way.

ALL THINGS FREELY GIVEN

This is a fundamental aspect of Paul's understanding of the cross, perhaps summarized best in this profound verse: "He who did not spare His own Son, but delivered Him up for us all, how shall He not with Him also freely give us all things?" (Romans 8:32).

All things are given to us *with Him*—with this sacrificial Lamb who was delivered up to darkest death for us, with this beloved and holy Son whom the Father refused to spare. What the cross makes available to every believer is *everything*.

In your relationship to God, the cross defines and releases everything else.

Are you letting God define for you what He means by "all things"? Or are you somehow limiting God? "All things" is a phrase that you don't really get a handle on unless you meditate deeply on it in God's presence.

It's as if we stand before God and He points to the cross and says, "What more could I have done for you? The cross contains it all! If I freely gave up My beloved and holy Son for you, doesn't that *prove* I'll freely give you everything else with Him as well? Doesn't it prove I have adequate resources to give you in Christ, since I already freely gave Him for your sin?"

The cross *defines* everything else in your relationship to God, and it *releases* everything else in your relationship to God. No wonder Paul was so passionate to proclaim exclusively "the message of the cross" (1 Corinthians 1:17–18). No wonder he said he "determined not to know anything among you except Jesus Christ and Him crucified." He didn't need any other message. The truth of the crucified Christ includes *everything* we could ever truly need.

The burning desire in Paul's heart was to see believers receiving the incredible vastness of all that the cross releases on our behalf. This was so real to Paul that he was able and willing to endure everything for the gospel.

ALREADY IN PLACE

As you look carefully throughout the New Testament, you'll see again and again that everything coming our way from God is ours through Christ by way of the cross.

In the opening lines of his letter to the Ephesians, Paul asserts that God "has blessed us with every spiritual blessing in the heavenly places in Christ" (Ephesians 1:3). There it is again! Paul's favorite phrase. *In Christ.*

Look closely at what Paul is saying. God *"has* blessed us." In other words, it's already in place. It's operative, on-line. And it includes *"every* spiritual blessing." Everything God can possibly do for you, touching every area of your life, has already been made available to you in Christ.

When Paul speaks of these as "spiritual" blessings, he doesn't mean something unreal, but rather blessings that come from the utmost reality of His Spirit at work in the here and now, all according to the presence, power, and purpose of God. All this has been provided for you to be released on your behalf.

We know that this incredible fullness of blessing involved the cross because of what Paul goes on to say in this passage— "just as He chose us in Him before the foundation of the world, that we should be holy and without blame before Him in love" (1:4).

God purposed to make us holy and blameless *before the foundation of the world*—with the holiness and blamelessness of Christ that are impossible for us to share without the cross. God, who knows everything, knew in eternity past that we would sin and fall short of His wondrous glory. Yet He also knew before the world was even created that He would provide a way for sinners to be made righteous before Him in Christ!

He created us as creatures of free choice, a freedom that means we can choose to sin (though we cannot choose the consequences of our sins). God fully knew what the deadly consequences of our sin would be, yet from eternity He had already planned and purposed how He would resolve that tragedy—through the death of His Son. And that plan and purpose would include not just forgiveness, but the countless, lavish blessings of all righteousness and holiness. What a God! What a Savior!

BECAUSE OF CHRIST'S OWN FULLNESS

The apostle John had a wonderful way of stating it: "And from his fullness we have all received, grace upon grace" (John 1:16, ESV). Out of His fullness, we have fullness. In Colossians 2:9–10, Paul declares: "For in Him dwells all the fullness of the Godhead bodily"—then adds these words about you and me: "and *you are complete in Him,* who is the head of all principality and power."

That's pretty strong, isn't it? In our union with Christ Jesus, we're totally *complete*. So often we think, *I still lack something*. Our problem is one of belief. We haven't yet grasped the truth that God accomplished all that He says He accomplished in the cross.

Knowing He has provided for us so completely through the cross, imagine how greatly dishonoring it is to Him when we set all that aside and try to function instead in the flesh.

GRACE FOR ALL GODLINESS

The apostle Peter speaks as well to the fullness of blessing we have in Christ through the cross. We see it, for example, in how his second epistle begins:

> Grace and peace be multiplied to you in the knowledge of God and of Jesus our Lord, as His divine power has given to us all things that pertain to life and godliness, through the knowledge of Him who called us by glory and virtue. (2 Peter 1:2–3)

The first word here is *grace*—which we know pertains to God's undeserved provision for us. Peter goes on to emphasize what this grace brings our way, through God's enabling power: It means *"all things* that pertain to life and godliness." All these things are what God *"has* given"; He has *already* supplied everything required for us to live a holy life. Nothing is left out.

Peter's prayer for them might be summarized like this: "May everything God has already provided you through the cross of Christ—all the resources required for living a holy life that honors Him—may all this grow and expand and intensify in your life, along with the great peace that always goes with it."

PROVIDED AND PROMISED

In the next verse, Peter fully links this gracious provision with God's "exceedingly great and precious promises," the promises through which we become "partakers of the divine nature, having escaped the corruption that is in the world through lust" (2 Peter 1:4). These are the same promises which, as Paul reminds us, all find their "Yes" in Christ (2 Corinthians 1:20). God's provision has not only been fully given to us, but also specifically expressed and guaranteed for us in His written promises confirmed in every way by Christ and the cross.

So often we settle in with our sinful nature and decide we just can't help it.

Yet so often we settle in with our sinful nature and decide we "just can't help it." We think we're bound to function that way, because "that's just how we are." And so we end up canceling God's promises in practical effect.

Will you instead learn to recognize everything God has done for you, and take full advantage of it? Accept His complete provision and ask Him to help you understand and appropriate what He has supplied. Come to Him and say, "O Father in heaven, I know Your promises. I know You have made available everything I need to live a godly life—I know that all this is already mine. And yet I just don't fully grasp how to implement these blessings. *But if You'll show me, I will respond.*"

If you do that continually over a lifetime, you'll increasingly become all that God wants you to be, as His grace and peace are multiplied unto you.

LET GOD DEFINE "ALL THINGS"

Are you committed to learning what God's "everything" and His "all things" really mean in every aspect of your life? If you're not motivated to learn it for your own life, then learn it for your marriage, your family and friends, your place of ministry, your work, and for all your circumstances. In every area, allow God to define for you and show you the fullness of His provision.

Remember again the question Paul asks in Romans 8:32— "He who did not spare His own Son, but delivered Him up for us all, how shall He not with Him also freely give us all things?" This comes in the context of another "all things" statement: "We know that all things work together for good to those who love God, to those who are the called according to His purpose" (8:28).

We *can* know, we who have been called by God's mercy and grace, that God's "all things" includes every circumstance of our lives, no matter how painful. Even in our darkest moments we can read this passage with great humility and brokenness and say, "I know You have called me, Lord, and I do love You with all my heart." As you begin putting that together in your mind and heart, you can say with genuine confidence, "Because of these things, I know God is working all things together for good."

THE CROSS IS WHERE HE TOLD US

Never forget that the cross is the heartbeat of all this good that God works out even through our toughest circumstances. I have learned this in a way I'll never forget, and though I've spoken of it in earlier books, I take the risk of mentioning it again. It so often comes with freshness to me as a reminder of what God wants to do in every area of my life.

When our daughter had cancer at age sixteen, in the bewilderment of it all I sensed God asking me this simple question: "Henry, where was it that I told you I loved you, and loved you forever?"

"Well, Lord, it was at the cross."

Then He said, "Then place your daughter in front of the cross, so you'll never become disoriented to My love. The love I demonstrated on the cross will never change, so place your daughter there, and understand right now that the cross and My love was for such a time as this."

God wants us to put all our circumstances in front of the cross, because if we don't, we'll question His love when difficult circumstances arise in our marriage or family or health, or in our ministry or work or finances. We'll be asking Him (or at least thinking the question in our minds), "Lord, if You love me, why would You let this happen?"

But He answers, "It's not by circumstances that I've told you I loved you. I told you I loved you when My Son died for you. And no combination of difficult or bewildering circumstances will ever change any aspect of that love."

How great is the love of God, that He could have planned such a redemption…worked it out so perfectly in His Son… then made *all* the fruit of this activity fully available to you and me!

THE WAITING GIFTS IN THE GARAGE

If you've been through *Experiencing God,* you know the story about my oldest son Richard and the blue Schwinn bicycle

The Holy Spirit persuades us to ask specifically for that which God has already richly provided for us through the cross.

I bought him as his sixth birthday approached. That's what I wanted him to have. But I also wanted to make sure that *he* wanted it. So I hid the bike in the garage, then took upon myself the task of making the kind of remarks and suggestions to convince Richard that a blue Schwinn bicycle was just what he needed.

"Richard," I eventually asked him, "what would you like most for your birthday?"

"Oh, Dad, I'd like a blue Schwinn bike."

"Well, son, I think you might get one."

You can understand the joy in my heart. I knew what I had freely prepared to give him, and now this was exactly what he expressed as his desire.

The Holy Spirit is like that—persuading us to ask specifically for that which God has already richly provided for us through the cross of Christ. That's the work of the Holy Spirit—to help us ask as we should, because "we do not know what we should pray for as we ought" (Romans 8:26).

What are these gifts in God's garage? They are unimaginable good: "Eye has not seen, nor ear heard, nor have entered into the heart of man the things which God has prepared for those who love Him. But God has revealed them to us through His Spirit" (1 Corinthians 2:9–10). His garage is full of the blessings He has already prepared, and the Spirit's assignment is to convince us to ask for them and to help us fully understand what they are: "Now we have received, not the spirit of the world, but the Spirit who is from God, that we might know the things that have been freely given to us by God" (1 Corinthians 2:12).

Jesus tells us, "Whatever you ask the Father in My name He will give you" (John 16:23). He can make that promise because the blessings we're to request in His will and in His name, through the Spirit's help, are already prepared and ready to distribute, as we respond to the Spirit in prayer.

DRAW NEAR

Because of the cross, we have "boldness to enter the Holiest by the blood of Jesus" (Hebrews 10:19). Now we can actually approach God's holy presence by His Spirit through prayer. In fact, we're encouraged to do exactly that without delay and without restriction: "Let us draw near with a true heart in full assurance of faith" (10:22); "Let us therefore come boldly to the throne of grace, that we may obtain mercy and find grace to help in time of need" (4:16).

How incredible! God has given you the go-ahead to enter the holiest place in existence, His very presence.

As you consistently do that, you honor Him. And don't

you suppose it must be terribly dishonoring if we have access to God's holy presence, purchased at the cost of the life of His own Son, and yet seldom go there? Surely a moment awaits when God will say to those who did not seek His presence, "Let Me tell you what *could have been* in your life, if you'd only come. But you didn't. You never came. You treated your prayer life as only a religious requirement." Don't let that tragedy be yours.

VICTORY OVER THE ENEMY

Christ's Total Defeat of Satan

*He raised Him from the dead and seated Him at His
right hand in the heavenly places, far above all
principality and power and might and dominion,
and every name that is named, not only in this age
but also in that which is to come.*

EPHESIANS 1:20–21

Spiritual warfare has become a hot topic in many Christian circles. Many believers give the subject great emphasis, avidly snapping up as many books on the subject as possible (from a vast and growing assortment).

But the victory in that war has already been won.

The Christian never works *toward* victory, he always works *from* victory.

Paul wants believers to understand that "all the fullness of the Godhead" dwells bodily in Christ, and that we are therefore "complete in Him, who is the head of all principality and power" (Colossians 2:9–10). He wants to expand our comprehension of all that God finished and provided in the cross—defeating sin and death and hell, and overcoming the

> *The cross and the resurrection brought about the complete, total defeat of all evil whatsoever.*

"spiritual hosts of wickedness in the heavenly places" (Ephesians 6:12). Throughout his epistles, Paul wants us to fully appropriate Christ's victory in our own lives through His Spirit. All the victory over evil that God accomplished in the death and resurrection of His Son is fully available to you and me.

When you come to the Truth, you'll come face to face with the reality of what God accomplished in Christ on the cross and in the resurrection. The cross and the resurrection brought about the complete, total defeat of evil in any and every form.

KNOWING YOU'RE THE WINNER

A liar and a deceiver, just as Jesus warned us (John 8:44), Satan tries to get Christians to believe that a host of demonic forces and powers are running rampant against us. He wants us to get caught up in the idea that somehow we ourselves have to win the battle against them. *But we don't.* Christ already defeated them, the same Jesus Christ who fully dwells in the lives of believers.

So when a demonic force comes to threaten a believer's life, you can imagine the conversation:

Christ tells the demon, "I defeated you."

"I know it," the demon says.

"Then why have you come against one of My children?"

"Because," the enemy answers, *You* know I'm defeated, and *I* know I'm defeated, but this person here doesn't realize it."

When you fully grasp, however, what the Lord and the enemy already grasp, the result is that *you're* the winner, and you know it. The enemy can do nothing without God's permission, so never function as if he had unrestricted access to your life and no limits on attacking you. He does not. Nothing in the Scripture indicates that he does.

But can he deceive you? Yes—as he tried to do with Jesus in the desert. He may even quote Scripture (just as he did with Jesus), trying to get you to misunderstand God's Word and go against the truth of God.

READING THE WRONG BOOKS

So why do so many believers assume the victory has not been won? I'm afraid that it's often because of all the spiritual warfare books circulating in the Christian community, and all the unsound teaching that flourishes with them. These believers often fail to read and study the only essential Book, the one that really matters, which is God's holy Scripture.

As an English major in college, I studied John Milton's epic poem *Paradise Lost*. Written in the mid-1600s, it presents a picture of hell that became very popular in its day. For well over a century, most people's thinking about hell was based much more on *Paradise Lost* than it was on Scripture.

Something similar has happened in our day. Most

Christians' perception of spiritual warfare is based much less on Scripture than it is on popular Christian fiction titles. Many of these readers simply accept whatever popular notion about warfare is out there, and never think to test it carefully for accuracy against God's Word.

That Word tells us that Jesus, by His death on the cross, "disarmed principalities and powers" and "made a public spectacle of them" (Colossians 2:14–15). The picture Paul gives us in this verse is that of victorious Roman generals returning from battle, as they marched their chained and captured foes through the streets for everyone to see and to mock.

That's how radically and thoroughly our almighty God—in the total event of the cross—has dealt with every principality and power, every demon in hell, every spiritual enemy that could ever come against you. And you glorify God when you live out that truth in your life, revealing in your words and actions the nature, purposes, and ways of God.

More than Conquerors

"If God is for us, who can be against us?"

Paul's question in Romans 8:31 has perhaps the most obvious answer in all of Scripture. *God* is for you! It's a simple declaration, but so full of meaning. He's *for* us—and therefore who can be against us? Absolutely no one. No one in the heavens. No one on earth. No one in hell.

It's the cross that says, as nothing else can, that God is for us. "He who did not spare His own Son, *but delivered Him up for us all,* how shall He not with Him also freely give us all things?" (v. 32). Paul then goes on to explain how absolutely nothing—not even "angels nor principalities nor powers"—could ever "separate us from the love of God which is in Christ Jesus our Lord" (vv. 38–39).

When God does something, He does it thoroughly—exceeding abundantly above and beyond all that we could ask or think. And the victory in the cross that He has won for us over the forces of spiritual evil is an overwhelming and everlasting victory. As a result, we're not just conquerors...we are *"more than conquerors"* (v. 37).

> *If you can't tell the difference between spiritual warfare and God's discipline, you're in serious trouble.*

The victory is won, and no spiritual force can ever separate you from God's love in the cross of Christ. Never act as though they can! Live the victory He has won for you, and let the world see it being lived out in your life.

THE DEVIL'S WORK OR GOD'S DISCIPLINE?

Because the theme of spiritual warfare has been such a strong fad in the Christian community for a number of years, too many of God's people see everything negative in that light. But if you can't tell the difference between spiritual warfare and God's discipline of His children, you're in serious trouble.

Why is that?

Because so often we forget the clear truth in Hebrews 12:5: "For whom the Lord loves He *chastens,* and *scourges* every son whom He receives." The God of the universe chastens and scourges *every one* of His children—and He does it *because* of His love for them. And it isn't some light slap-on-the-hand correction—but rather something that is indeed "painful" (12:11).

Would it not then be important for us to understand what this discipline from God is like, and why He does it—so we're able to recognize it when it happens to us? Otherwise, in the spiritual climate of today, when we encounter that painful discipline we'll simply think the devil is responsible for it, instead of realizing this is what God Himself is doing.

When God disciplines His children, it's far more severe than anything Satan ever does to us. Satan is severely limited in what he's permitted to do, and he has to ask permission when he takes action against the people of God. Our enemy never has an open-ended opportunity to do whatever he wants with believers.

Contrast that with what God does. Nowhere in Scripture do I see that Satan ever destroyed the people of God, but when you look at the biblical record of God's discipline, He *did* destroy His people. In Old Testament times He crushed the nation of Israel and sent them into captivity; then He burned and razed Jerusalem and overthrew the nation of Judah, sending them into captivity as well. Centuries later, God totally destroyed the city of Jerusalem again only a few short decades after Jesus Christ ascended into heaven.

So we need to be very consciously aware of the seriousness of attributing the activity of our Father God to Satan. If we keep on blaming everything negative or painful in our lives on the devil, we may very well miss the good and loving work of discipline and training God seeks to accomplish in our lives.

CHAPTER 12

TAKE UP YOUR CROSS

The Cost of Dealing with Sin

Christ died for our sins...

1 CORINTHIANS 15:3

We began this book recalling how Jesus spoke often in the Gospels of our need to take up our cross (see Matthew 10:38; 16:24; Mark 8:34; 10:21; Luke 9:23; 14:27).

We rarely think of those Scriptures as referring to our dealing with sin. When we hear the Savior say, "Take up your cross," we tend to think mostly of our need simply to count the cost of following Him and of doing God's will in our life. Certainly, we have to do that. But I believe there is more here. I think He specifically wants us to recognize, accept, and bear the cost involved in *dealing personally with our sin.*

THE CROSS WAS ABOUT SIN

To Jesus, the cross meant obedience to His Father. Even more specifically, however, it meant obedience to God *as God deals with sin.* We cannot understand the cross of Jesus Christ without grasping that it's primarily about God's confrontation with man's sin. And if the cross of Jesus Christ dealt with sin, then the cross in the Christian's life must deal with sin also.

If you more fully understand the meaning of the cross, you realize that to take up our cross as Jesus tells us to means that you deliberately choose to radically deal with sin in your life.

Confrontation against sin is central to the Christian life.

We've stated before how absolutely central the cross is in the Christian life. For this reason, the Christian's confrontation against sin is also central in the Christian life. In fact, the whole issue of personal holiness lies at the very center of our walk with Jesus Christ, as we'll explore more thoroughly later.

Sin in a believer's life is what keeps that individual from practicing and experiencing God's will. That's why you must make a radical commitment in your heart and mind to constantly and vigilantly deal with sin in your life.

TAKE UP YOUR CROSS, OR YOU'RE UNWORTHY TO FOLLOW HIM

Let's specifically examine a few of those passages where Jesus mentions taking up our cross.

Jesus said, "He who does not take his cross and follow after Me is not worthy of Me" (Matthew 10:38). Let those words linger in your mind for a time of meditation before the Lord.

He's telling us that for you and me to even think of following Him in a worthy manner, the cross must be central in our life—which means dealing with sin must be central in our life.

How could it be otherwise? How could we be indifferent to sin when we know how radically God had to deal with the sin issue—at an unimaginable cost to Himself and His Son—on the cross?

It's unthinkable to say, "Father, thank You for laying the sin of the world on Your Son…but please don't talk to me about sin in my life. I just want to have the joy of following You."

TAKE UP YOUR CROSS, OR YOU CANNOT EVEN BE HIS DISCIPLE

Jesus also said, "Whoever does not bear his cross and come after Me cannot be My disciple" (Luke 14:27).

Here's a statement that leaves us no room for maneuver.

There's nothing halfway about it; either we take up our cross, or it's absolutely impossible to be His disciple. Would it not be important, then, that we understand completely and profoundly what it means to bear our cross?

Jesus never hides the terms of discipleship, and the terms He lays down are non-negotiable. They're absolutes—and it's time for us to let the living Christ once again define the terms of discipleship. The essence of a follower of Jesus Christ is one who has dealt with and continually deals with sin in a radical manner in his or her life.

You might say, "Henry, that sounds awfully absolute."

It does. But never forget how God looks upon sin. It's awful to Him. It's an unspeakable affront. For us to call ourselves disciples of Jesus Christ and dilly-dally with sin in our lives is abhorrent to God! And it must be unthinkable on our part.

> *To call ourselves disciples of Jesus Christ and have an indifference to sin is abhorrent to God.*

There must be a cross in the Christian's life, and if you fill that word *cross* full of New Testament meaning, you realize that you must take up that cross in regard to sin in your life. You must come to a particular kind of obedience to your Lord in regard to renouncing sin, or you will not truly be following Him.

DEALING RADICALLY WITH SIN

Let me say it once more: *The cross of Christ has to do exclusively with sin;* that's why it's a part of history! If God had somehow chosen not to deal with sin, the event of the cross would never have happened…and we would have been lost in our sins.

Understanding this, you and I cannot accurately look at the cross without a radical understanding of the nature of sin, and the cost to God to forgive us of our sin. That process is what we have begun together in this book—stirring our minds and hearts toward understanding a little more of the nature of what is meant by that word *cross*.

Remember that as God dealt with sin in the cross, He dealt with it *radically*. How could it be less in our lives? God doesn't deal thoroughly with sin on the cross and then just barely touch sin in your life.

In the next few chapters, we want to explore how to apply the context of the cross to your life, as you consider what it means to deal radically with sin. As we do, I invite you to let the Holy Spirit bring to your remembrance some of the things you've read in previous chapters. Keep in mind especially the profound truth Paul revealed to us when he wrote in 2 Corinthians 5:21, "He made Him who knew no sin to be sin for us, that we might become the righteousness of God in Him."

Ask God to open your eyes to a fresh understanding of these amazing truths.

CHAPTER 13

WHAT OUR SIN REALLY IS

Why God Cannot Ignore It

Every one shall die for his own iniquity.

JEREMIAH 31:30

There is a strong need in our day to come to a fresh understanding of what the Bible means by sin and sin's effect on our lives.

In light of the special attention this topic needs, I want to address this with you in a personal and practical way.

SIN IS AS BAD AS GOD SAYS IT IS

God wasn't playing games with sin when He allowed His Son to be crucified. Sin is as bad as God tells us it is, with eternal consequences every bit as horrible as God describes them. We must never forget: Sin is so serious to the mind of God that He was willing to take His only Son—who knew no sin and lived in perfect holiness—and to *make* Him to be sin for us.

Roman crucifixion was the most cruel form of physical death mankind has ever devised, and Jesus had to endure that. But this was not the greatest tragedy of the cross. The greatest tragedy of it is what God did when He laid all the sin of the world on His Son. By this means, God dealt thoroughly and radically with sin so His justice and His holiness would be upheld. All that would be required to deal with sin fell upon His Son in an indescribably dreadful blow.

So let me ask you again. Do you suppose there's any possibility, after God dealt with sin so radically through His Son, that once He brings us into union with Christ there'll be any particular sin in our lives that He isn't really concerned about? Are there sins He will choose to simply wink at, or ignore?

God intends to deals radically with every sin in the life of every person He brings to Himself.

No, there's no possibility of that. God intends to deal radically with every sin in the life of every person He brings to Himself.

Yet many believers will read a statement such as Romans 6:14—"Sin shall not have dominion over you"—and respond by saying or thinking, "Well, I don't really know what that verse means, but what I do know is that I keep on sinning." They say it with a casualness that frightens me. When the Christian treats sin casually, we're in a disaster.

OUR SIN OFFENDS GOD'S HOLINESS

By the very nature of God's absolute holiness He *must* confront your sin. He cannot overlook it, nor will He; His holy nature demands that He deal with it. He has an utter hatred of sin that is absolute and irreversible, and this is true of *every* sin in our lives.

That's why you must fully respond throughout your life to what God has done in the cross to reconcile you. By His nature He must deal with your sin, and either you consciously and continually let Him keep doing that in what He accomplished *in His Son* on the cross—or else God must deal with it *in you*. One way or the other, God will deal with your sin, because His nature requires it.

I always begin my day by asking the Spirit of God to keep me as sensitive to sin in my heart, life, mind, and will as I can possibly be. *It was my sin that crucified my Savior!* I do not have the audacity to say, "God, I thank You and praise You for who You are" while sin runs unchecked in my life. That would only be hypocrisy.

REMINDERS OF OUR SIN

Early in this book we explored how the cross was in the mind and heart of God before He ever began to create. And as the history of His people unfolds from the book of Genesis onward, we find God using every conceivable means to cause His people to understand the seriousness of sin and His loving provision to forgive them, restore them, and continue His blessing upon them.

The whole sacrificial system in the Old Testament was a clear and powerful reminder of sin's seriousness and the cost of forgiveness—that without the shedding of blood there was no remission of sin. If you were in Jerusalem at that time, then day after day you would see sacrificial animals being slain upon the temple altar, with blood splattered and flowing everywhere.

As you picture that scene, you may find yourself thinking, *That's awfully gory.*

But so is sin.

And if you lose sight of the severity of sin and of the magnitude of eternity and of the holiness of God, you'll start feeling sorry for the sheep and goats getting slain instead of thinking about these sacrifices as God intended. He wants us to examine our own hearts with an ever-stronger sensitivity to sin.

> *You may think,*
> *"That's awfully gory."*
> *But so is sin.*

He wants us to hate sin as He does.

The same forgetfulness can happen when we partake of communion, the Lord's Supper. Paul says that when we come to eat of the bread and drink of the cup, we must first *examine* ourselves (1 Corinthians 11:27–29). Ask the Spirit of God to run His plumb line across your life to see if there is any relationship you've wounded, or anything in word or deed by which you have offended God—anything at all in your life that God would call sin. And if, when you examine yourself in this way by God's light, you find sin, then what you should do immediately before coming to the Lord's Supper is *confess* that sin.

We need to hear Jesus saying, "This is My body which is broken *for you*" (11:24). And why was it broken? Because of your sin. Hear Him say as well, "This cup is the new covenant in My blood" (v. 25)—His blood that seals the agreement God made with His children to provide a covering of atonement for our sins. Let the Lord's Supper always remind you of the seriousness of your sin.

OUR SIN IS REBELLION

The Bible uses a number of terms that describe sin and its essence from various perspectives.

One of those words is *rebellion*—a spirit that rebels against God's will. A rebellious spirit in the heart of a child of God is gross sin! When you're stubbornly resisting the Lord's guidance or authority, you may tell yourself, *I'm just wrestling with God.* You may even think it's cute to argue with Him in this way, and to tell Him, "Lord, don't You understand?" But the truth is that you're rebelling against Him. And as Samuel said to King Saul, "Rebellion is as the sin of witchcraft, and stubbornness is as iniquity and idolatry" (1 Samuel 15:23).

There are some who love to claim that it's "normal" to resist and question God; but I say that for those Christians, *sin* is what's normal in their life.

I cannot remember a time when there was a rebellious spirit in my heart against God that led me to disobey something I clearly knew He was asking me to do. I fear God enough to know that perfect knowledge never makes a mistake. Nor does perfect love. So if I know God in His perfect wisdom and love is directing me, it doesn't cross my mind to argue with His instructions.

Once God makes His will clear to us, we have a very narrow window in which to respond. We don't have all the time in the world. If we delay our obedience too long, we may lose a great deal; God sees such a delay as rebellion, and He does not reward rebellion.

Perhaps you went through a time of rebellion against God in your past before choosing to obey Him, and now you might be tempted to think, *Well, God is still using me, even though I rebelled against Him before.* That may certainly be true, by the Lord's mercy and grace—but you'll never know what could have been! Because of the length of time it took you to get around to saying yes, there are great dimensions of God's activity you'll never know or experience.

If we delay our obedience too long, we may lose a great deal.

Remember, you don't want to be receiving God's minimum; you want to be enjoying His maximum. And that requires a heart that knows Him, loves Him, recognizes His voice, and understands how the only worthy answer to Him is, "Yes, Lord!"

OUR SIN IS LAWLESSNESS

Sin is also called "lawlessness" in Scripture. "Whoever commits sin also commits lawlessness, and sin is lawlessness" (1 John 3:4).

Let me break that word down: Sin is *law-less-ness.* The practicing sinner is lawless, without God's law. In other words, it means you're trying to live without any standard of God's Word to judge your decisions. You're living outside the clear directives of His Word. It may be because you're unfamiliar with God's ways. You haven't read and studied His Word with passion, seeking to apply it to your daily life.

A Christian who loves the Lord sets about immediately to

immerse his or her life in God's ways and purposes as specifically shown in Scripture. His laws and commands are the standard to help us identify sin. You may say, "Well, I just don't have time." What is it, then, that demands your allegiance and time above your relationship with your God and Savior? I would suggest that anything in your life that has preempted that place that belongs to Him has become an idol.

God has the right to expect that His child will seek to know the will of the Father.

God alone is God; He has the right to give you directives, and He has the right to expect that His child will seek to know and understand His will.

We may try to justify our waywardness by saying, "Well, Lord, I didn't know it was wrong."

"You could have known," He answers, "but you chose not to."

"But nobody told me," we might protest.

He replies, "If you were listening, My Word and the Holy Spirit would have told you."

Even on the human level, ignorance of the law is never an excuse; how much more is that true on God's level!

Our lives are a product of the choices we've made, and no amount of reading in books written by others will ever be a substitute for your personal study of the Bible. Nor can reading the biblical study done by others ever replace the study *you* must do on your own in the Scriptures, with the Spirit of God as your Teacher.

Jesus said, "I do not seek My own will but the will of the Father who sent Me" (John 5:30). He said, "I always do those things that please Him" (8:29). In order to live this way, Jesus immersed His life in Scripture all the way through. He was always quoting Scripture and using Scripture to guide Him. How can we claim to be His followers and do less? To fail to learn and observe His guidelines is sin, and it is lawlessness.

OUR SIN IS DEADLY

Another biblical word for sin is *transgression,* a term that means exceeding or overstepping a limit or boundary. God has given His people clear boundaries we aren't to cross, and if we cross over any of them or ignore them, we "transgress" His law and earn His wrath. God sent the nation of Israel into captivity "because they did not obey the voice of the LORD their God, but *transgressed* His covenant and all that Moses the servant of the LORD had commanded; and they would neither hear nor do them" (2 Kings 18:12).

Yet another word in Scripture for sin is *iniquity,* which has to do especially with deviation or a perversion or twisting of standards. Psalm 64:6 tells us how sinners "devise iniquities," and how they boast, "We have perfected a shrewd scheme."

There are many other words as well—*injustice, wickedness, unrighteousness, evil deeds,* and more—a great variety of terms that God uses to keep impressing upon us the deep and comprehensive repulsiveness of sin. And He fully warns us that all of it brings *death.*

There's a well-known Old Testament verse you may recall—does it say, "The soul who sins will struggle"? Or, "The soul who sins will have difficulty"? No; it says, "The soul who sins shall *die*" (Ezekiel 18:20). Sin is deadly serious to God.

Does that deadliness hold for Christians as well as for unbelievers? Absolutely! The soul that continues to sin will know the withering and dying of a relationship with God, and a shrinking capacity to receive and enjoy His purpose and will.

Over the years I've seen and talked with many believers who in the past had known God's call to ministry and missions, but who then died to the call God gave them. I have a real heart to help them, but so often it seems that no amount of repentance on their part can restore what has been lost. They say, "I've repented, and God has forgiven me, but there's no door opening for me." What I ask them to consider is this: "Christ has closed the door for you that once was open, and Scripture says that what He closes, no man can open. So I'd be fearful to try and force it open if I were you."

Christ has closed the door for you that once was open, and what He closes, no man can open.

Does this mean that in such a situation your life can be of no further use to God? Of course not. Your life can be of great use in God's purposes. But when you sin against God, there are some matters that die, matters that cannot be restored, though there may be other things of lesser importance that God will rearrange and reestablish for you. So we must be extremely careful that we don't ignore what the Scriptures say about sin, because the soul who sins will die.

It's not that the wages of sin is a limitation on life.

It's not that the wages of sin is some hindrance to your lifestyle.

No, "the wages of sin is death" (Romans 6:23). Death is sin's payoff, and that has always been true, from the very beginning. Remember God's warning to Adam about that one tree in Eden? "In the day that you eat of it *you shall surely die*" (Genesis 2:17).

OUR SIN AFFECTS EVERYONE AROUND US

All sin is deadly, and the deadening effect of our own sin goes beyond ourselves. The sin of Adam and Eve corrupted the entire human race for all history, and also put the whole cosmic universe out of joint. Someday all of creation will "be delivered from the bondage of corruption," but until that happens, "the whole creation groans" (Romans 8:21–22). Such were the consequences of the sin of one man and one woman! And if that was true for one act of disobedience by Adam and Eve, what do you suppose is the consequence of *your* sins?

You can never sin in private. You may be able to sin in secret, but you can't in private, because your sin will immediately affect everything around you. Your church, your family, your work— everything will to some degree be put out of joint because of your sin. You'll face obstacles that weren't there before, fresh hindrances and difficulties, and things just won't be the same.

Perhaps you're experiencing this kind of futility right now.

If so, you need to understand as well the good news that just as our sin affects those around us, so also our getting right with God will have tremendously positive effects all around us. A step of repentance and obedience can be the tremor that brings a huge movement of God and great freedom and release to many.

I know of one church in Canada where many had prayed for well over a year for God to move mightily. In that church were two deacons, who also happened to be brothers. Although they both served as leaders in that fellowship, there was sin between them that had broken their relationship. They rarely even spoke to one another. At the time they didn't grasp the full dimension or effect of their sin. They just knew that on the personal level, things were not right between them.

Then came the day when the Spirit moved in one brother's heart, and he rose from where he was seated on one side of the church and walked forward, head bowed, to confess his sin. At the same time, unknown to him, his brother on the other side of the room was convicted of his sin and came forward as well.

They literally fell into an embrace as they reached the altar in front, and before God and the entire church they repented in tears.

In the wake of this, a mother stood up at one side of the auditorium to speak publicly to her teenage daughter, seated some distance away. "I haven't been the mother I ought to be to you," she confessed. The mother and daughter went to each other and they, too, embraced in tears and were reconciled.

This went on with others as well, so that the church meeting lasted for hours. All throughout the little church family, people were getting right with God and reconciled with each other.

What had happened? God had restored two men to the relationship they ought to have had—and that restoration released a rush of freedom for everyone else to rightly respond to the Spirit's conviction as well. And though the two brothers

didn't realize it earlier, this freedom was being suppressed
because of their sin. They hadn't been
serious about the Word of God and
the kind of relationships it requires in
the church, because the Bible makes
it clear that there is *no* justification
for ever being unreconciled with a
Christian brother or sister.

*A single moment of our
public repentance can bring
great freedom of repentance
for many others.*

If we hold on to sin in our heart and life, it can deepen
and prolong a hardness on the hearts of those around us. But
a single moment of our public repentance can be used by God
to bring conviction and great freedom of repentance for many,
many others.

THE REPENTANCE REQUIRED

If God in this moment is bringing some sin to mind and the
Holy Spirit is convicting your heart, there's only one way to
deal with it. There must be *repentance*. Just asking God to
forgive you isn't enough. Simply asking for His forgiveness
isn't the same as repentance.

Repentance is acknowledging that what I've done is serious
to God, that in some area of life I've actually been going in an
opposite direction from where He wants me to go, and my
direction is a wrong one. So I make a choice—a conscious
choice—to turn around and go in *His* direction, because Jesus
Christ is the *way* and the truth and the life. I flee to the Savior
and ask Him to help me live in a way that's the opposite of how

I've been living.

In this moment, you may need to begin your repentance by telling Him, "Lord, I've been neglecting the serious study of Your Word, and that is sin! I've known what You say about Your Word, and what You've wanted from me in response to that, but I haven't obeyed it. I've sinned against *You,* and the impact of that is immeasurable. Lord, I repent of that in my mind and my heart, and with Your Spirit as my Convicter and Helper and Guide, I will turn around, and I will not transgress what I know to be the will of God."

CHAPTER 14

YOUR SIN AND THE CROSS OF CHRIST

The Incomprehensible Wonder of Our Salvation

> *Grace to you and peace from God the Father*
> *and our Lord Jesus Christ, who gave Himself for our sins,*
> *that He might deliver us from this present evil age,*
> *according to the will of our God and Father,*
> *to whom be glory forever and ever. Amen.*

GALATIANS 1:3–5

Considering the deadly seriousness of our sin brings us once again to the foot of the cross. In the cross, God dealt with all that sin *has done,* all that sin *can do,* and all that sin really is.

The death of Jesus was *for your sin.* That's why I can get nervous when I hear people say they've accepted Christ into their heart and will now go to heaven, but make no reference to their sin. And it's why I'm so concerned when I see tracts and evangelism methods that don't mention repentance of sin.

Impossible! The whole meaning of salvation is that God deals radically with our sin!

I'm afraid there are many who've never truly turned from their sin, yet believe they are saved. But if they have never dealt with sin in their lives, if they have never repented and turned away from their sin, salvation is impossible.

In salvation, a man or woman is delivered out of the kingdom of darkness and placed into the kingdom of God's dear Son. The change is so radical that Scripture speaks of it as becoming a new creation—the old is gone, and everything becomes new. So my question for those who say they're new believers is this: Have you been radically born from above by letting the Father deal with *your* sin in His Son Jesus, when He laid that sin upon Him on the cross? Have you believed what God says about this, and fully exchanged the sin in your life for the righteousness of Christ?

GOD'S DEEPEST HEART REVEALED TO MANKIND

The issue of our need to escape from sin and its effects is so serious to God that He uses a multitude of terms and word pictures in Scripture to describe and portray it.

He talks about our need for a *ransom.*

He talks about our need to be *justified.*

He talks about our need to be *reconciled.*

He uses all manner of figures of speech and terminology to indicate that which is *not* right with us because of our sin, and yet which must be made right.

For God to remain God, His holiness requires that the penalty of our sin remain upon us—or else He must somehow deal with it Himself on our behalf. And that's exactly what He chose to do. God Himself had to come and stand between His own justice and the punishment we rightfully deserve. Simply because He loved us, God "has reconciled us to Himself through Jesus Christ" (2 Corinthians 5:18).

The way of our salvation—and our need for it—is the most profoundly serious thing that the loving heart of God has ever revealed to mankind. God so loved the world that He released and literally chose to give His only begotten Son, that whoever would believe in Him would not...*perish!* What would have happened had He not given His Son? We would have perished with no hope whatsoever, with no possibility of ever making up for the wrong we've done to a Holy God in our rebellion and lawlessness and transgression. We would have been totally lost, without God, without hope, without recourse.

God Himself had to come and stand between His own justice and the punishment we rightfully deserve.

When Peter writes about Christ's suffering and the reason for it, he tells us, "You were like sheep going astray" (1 Peter 2:25). One of the characteristics of sheep is that they can't find their way home! Sheep are of such a nature that they wander aimlessly, and once they're lost they don't have the instinct to return home. A dog can find its way home from many miles away. So can a cat, an ox, a pigeon, or a donkey. Even a salmon can find its way back to the pool where it was spawned, after months at sea. But a sheep doesn't have the capacity to find its way back.

And that's what God says we are like—lost lambs. Human beings are totally incapable of finding salvation on their own. God had to provide that salvation on His own, and this is what He has done.

FREEDOM TO BE RESTORED

Remember again Paul's statement in 2 Corinthians 5:21 of what God the Father did to His Son: "He made Him who knew no sin to be sin for us." No combination of the wisest and most spiritual-minded people, no matter how many, could ever plumb the depths of what that verse really means.

Frequently in my prayer times, I've asked God to open my understanding to those words. And there are times when I sense He has brought me to the very fringes of understanding. In those moments, I've found myself weeping with inexpressible pain just thinking about it.

The blackness of that moment is something no one can describe.

The spotless Son of God, the One who dwelt in eternity with His Father, and who was loved so profoundly and intimately by His Father beyond any description of love we could ever comprehend—this is the One whom God gave over.

And His Son freely responded, "Not My will but Thine be done," so that the agony of spiritual death began to overwhelm Him and carry Him into the deepest recesses of God's judgment upon sin.

God *made Him* sin.

God dealt with sin in an unrelenting wrath that fell on His Son, and the blackness of that moment is something no one can describe. Absolutely none of the terror of it was withheld from His Son, so that everything required for our salvation could be accomplished.

In Genesis 22, when Abraham was ready to drive a knife into the body of his son Isaac, God stayed Abraham's hand and did not let death fall upon the boy. But when it came to His own Son, there was no holding back. All that the holiness and justice of God required to fall upon us for our sin, fell instead upon His Son.

My heart is overwhelmed, knowing that all this was to deal with *my* sin and to make it possible for *me* to be forgiven— so that God could put a seal over my life and my soul that says, *Paid in Full—Now Free to Be Restored.* Have you allowed yourself to really feel this and know it in your soul?

What a treasure of meaning the cross becomes in the heart of the Christian's life! How could anyone ever really argue with a God who loves us that much? How could anyone ever fuss over any demand He makes of our life? For we owe it *all* to Him!

That's why the Christian is to live a cross-centered life.

SAVED BY GRACE THROUGH FAITH

We can't save ourselves from our sin, but God Himself has dealt with it and has told us how to respond to His activity. We're to *believe* Him and release to Him our lives, including all our sin. On that basis we're counted as righteous, just as

Abraham was: "Abraham believed God, and it was accounted to him for righteousness" (Romans 4:3).

Faith is always based on what you know, not on what you don't know, and all that Abraham *knew,* he believed—with a confident trust and reliance upon God. In response, God counted Abraham's belief as righteousness.

It's the same with you and me, though on this side of the cross, we possess more knowledge than Abraham did. As we now actively *believe* what we have seen and known, God accounts to us His righteousness over our lives. And that righteousness is complete and full.

"Who shall bring a charge against God's elect?" Paul asks in Romans 8:33. "It is God who justifies." No one can bring you into the courtroom of God and make a charge against you that would prevent your salvation, because the Judge of that court already declares you "not guilty." He's declared you righteous, and He does so on the basis of your acceptance of and faith in what He's accomplished in the death of His Son on your behalf.

It's not your faith that saves you, it is God's grace, His provision. Faith is simply the response God seeks to find in each of us in order to apply His effective provision. I often hear people say, "I'm saved by faith." But the truth is that we're saved *by* grace *through* faith—"For by grace you have been saved through faith" (Ephesians 2:8). We cast ourselves on the mercy of God, the love of God, and the grace of God, but we cannot be saved by this mercy and love and grace without faith. Our belief is absolutely essential.

IMMERSED INTO CHRIST'S
DEATH AND BURIAL

Effective faith also understands that when we enter a relationship with Jesus Christ, we're *immersed* into His death and into His burial. This is what Paul tells us in the early verses of Romans 6— and I don't think I'm violating Scripture when I say that this is much more to Paul than some theological position.

Down through the years, there are Christians whose lives have profoundly affected their world, and who have testified— quietly and reverently—of how, in a moment almost beyond description, the God of the universe took them into the death of our Lord and even into His burial. There they looked into the mouth of hell and saw what hell was like—how real, how personal, how awful, how permanent, how separating.

This is much more to Paul than some theological position.

This is a moment and an experience that only God can grant to someone by His Spirit, and I believe He grants it only to those who *know* that He's standing there beside them, because otherwise they would not be able to handle the sight of it.

Let me ask you: Do you believe God wants you to more fully understand what it means to die with Christ and to be buried with Christ, and to grasp more fully what happened to the Son of God in this experience? And as you began to understand this more and more—do you think you could ever be indifferent or casual toward sin in your life?

WE DIED TO SIN

Our immersion into Christ's death and burial is so complete that Paul tells us we actually "died to sin" (6:2). He says clearly, "Reckon yourselves to be dead indeed to sin" (Romans 6:11).

Peter says it as well—that Jesus suffered and died "that we, *having died to sins,* might live for righteousness" (1 Peter 2:24).

So what does it mean to be dead to sin? Well, it means that you're dead to sin!

Yet when I direct people to verses like these, they almost always respond, "But of course we all sin," as if those verses had no ultimate meaning that counts for anything. The way we should be responding to those passages, however, is going to God and saying, "Lord, what does this mean?" Then we allow Him to take those Scriptures and pour them over our heart until we truly understand that in the cross *we die to sin.*

As we discovered earlier, death for the Lord Jesus was not just a cessation of physical life, but something much more profound and deep. It was so deep that by His death the Lord Jesus actually defeated death. He took upon Himself all the darkness and the blackness of the sin of the entire world, and emerged victorious from the tomb.

Paul says we were immersed in the Christ's death and burial *for a reason:* "that just as Christ was raised from the dead by the glory of the Father, even *so we also should walk in newness of life*" (Romans 6:3–5). Not, "so we also should walk in the same old life," but that we could experience actual *newness* of life! And that is what we want to look at next.

CHAPTER 15

FREEDOM FROM SIN

Replacing Active Sin with Active Righteousness

The Spirit of the LORD is upon Me...
He has sent Me to heal the brokenhearted,
to proclaim liberty to the captives...

LUKE 4:18

Paul prays in Ephesians 1 that we will know a radical experience of God's power—"the exceeding greatness of His power toward us who believe, according to the working of His mighty power which He worked in Christ when He raised Him from the dead (Ephesians 1:19–20). And what is that power for?

It is primarily power over sin.

A MAN REBORN

Years ago, when I was a pastor for a church in the East Bay area near San Francisco, I received a phone call one day from a woman who named a certain couple and asked if I was their pastor. I answered that the wife of this couple was indeed a member of our church, but the husband was not. In fact, he wasn't a Christian.

The woman told me she was a neighbor to this couple, and looking out her window she had just seen the wife carrying her baby in her arms and jumping a fence, with the husband coming after her with a butcher knife.

I immediately went to their neighborhood to see what I could do. I found the husband, and it was obvious he'd been drinking. He also had a huge cut down his face from some brawl he'd been in. I took him back home, and sat across the kitchen table from him, while his wife held her baby and cowered in a back room.

He began to weep over his sin and over how he'd treated his family.

As a pastor I never hesitated to work with people hooked on alcohol. I had come across a great many of them, and had seen how the power of the gospel could utterly and miraculously transform them.

As I spoke with this man, he began to weep over his sin and over how he'd treated his family. It didn't take long for him to put his faith in Christ. He was wonderfully saved—radically saved, as time would prove. He and his wife would become a model couple in their neighborhood, and the husband would be a model of kindness and gentleness.

But that was still in the future as I stepped out of the kitchen that day to ask the man's wife to join us there. "Your husband has something to say to you," I told her. I wanted him to tell her what had happened to him. I never try to say something for others when it's best that they speak for themselves.

You can well imagine the wife's reaction. She was deeply frightened, and hesitant to go in. But I told her, "You never have to be afraid of him again."

When she finally entered the kitchen, her husband broke down once more in tears. "I've sinned against God," he said, "and I've sinned against you. But I want you to know that God has forgiven me, and I've asked Jesus into my life to be the Lord of my life. I want you to forgive me. I want to make up the time I've lost and to be the kind of husband you've always wanted."

It was a wonderful, glorious time.

Joy for the First Time

About a week later, our church sponsored an outing at a lake, and this man and his wife joined us. We hadn't been there long when he asked me, "Henry, do you hear those birds?"

"I do."

Then he told me, "For the first time I'm hearing birds sing." He was hearing and seeing things that filled him with an incredible joy he'd never known before. That's what happens when Christ cleanses you.

Now do you think this man would have been enjoying the sounds of those birds singing if at that moment he was still harboring anger toward his wife, or still craving a bottle of alcohol? I don't think so. It was freedom from sin that made his joy possible.

Sin has a way of deadening a person to the possibility of enjoying life's true blessings.

Sin robs you of life.

But the cross of Christ has power to destroy that deadening influence and to restore you to the fullness of life God intends for you, so that you see and hear and experience all that's there for you as a child of God.

God wants to lead you into things you've never before seen or heard or experienced.

The salvation of God carries that dimension for all of us. He wants to lead you into things you've never before seen or heard or experienced, through the power of being freed from sin to live fully in the center of His will.

REMEMBER SIN'S EFFECT, AND REMEMBER GRACE

While I was serving as a pastor in the East Bay area, every month I would take a group from our church on a ministry trip to San Francisco's skid row. I wanted our people never to forget what sin can do, and to also see what the grace of God can do—and we all need to remember both.

In one evangelistic meeting we had there, I prayed with a huge black man who I found out later had once been a professional boxer, but whose life had been derailed by alcohol. He'd lost everything—his wife, his children, his boxing career. I shared with him the good news of God's provision for his life through the cross. When he opened his life to allow Christ to forgive him and change him, it was an astounding moment—for me as well as for him. I thought *my* life was about to end, because this gigantic mass of muscle embraced me, and almost hugged the life out of me. I was thinking, *Lord, I'm coming home.*

I never saw a man more full of joy or more completely set free. He experienced victory over what sin had done to him. Sin's power was broken, and he no longer had to submit to alcohol's control. He was free.

THE TOTALITY OF GOD'S DELIVERANCE

Are you seeing the fuller picture of everything God did in that huge event called the cross?

The salvation God provides is totally thorough. He hasn't left anything out. God has already taken care of all the wrong things you've done in your past—all the times you ignored Him, all the times you didn't serve Him, all the times you were self-centered—God has dealt with all that, as well as giving you everlasting life to begin experiencing *now,* in the present: "We have passed from death to life" (1 John 3:14).

And having done all this, here's what God is counting on from you: That in the full knowledge of your forgiveness, you'll forever take up arms against sin and be victorious in the fight.

This victory is possible because the cross deals not only with the *penalty* for our sins, the cross also overcomes the whole reality of our nature of sin. It is this nature that brings about specific sinful actions and attitudes in our lives. We can be assured that if the cross dealt radically with *sin* then the cross will also deal radically with *sins.*

Our sinful nature is the reason we commit specific sinful actions; *sin* is the reason for *sins* in our lives. Our sin nature is that controlling tendency that keeps drawing us away from

God. But when we become a Christian, we die to sin as the dominating factor in our behavior. In every area where we experience moral failure and addiction and defeat, in every area where we simply cannot help ourselves, we can now find absolute, radical victory over sin.

Do you sense again just how profound is God's plan to redeem us? It covers not only the specific sins we commit, but the core problem of sin which has permeated the whole of mankind.

Being born again brings an immediate and totally changed attitude toward sin.

A man or woman genuinely born again by the Spirit of God has experienced a radical transformation, bringing about an immediate and totally changed attitude toward sin.

NO LONGER PRACTICING SIN

The apostle John writes, "Whoever abides in Him [that is, in Christ] does not sin" (1 John 3:6).

Now there's a tough passage.

I suspect that our problem with this verse (as with many other "difficult" scriptures) is not that we *don't* understand what John is saying, but rather that we *do* understand it only too well—and don't like it.

Yes, it's a tough passage, and as we keep reading carefully in 1 John 3, it only gets tougher:

Whoever sins has neither seen Him [Christ] nor known Him. (v. 6)

Are you getting the impression here that when you enter into a relationship with Christ, He deals *decisively* with the presence of sin in your life? If that isn't happening, John insists, you haven't really known Him, because the essence of a relationship with Jesus Christ is what He does with your sin.

Well, it gets tougher. Listen carefully to John's words:

He who sins is of the devil. (v. 8)

And then comes this statement:

Whoever has been born of God does not sin. (v. 9)

John doesn't say that the person born of God doesn't sin very much, or doesn't sin as much as he once did, but rather that he *does not sin*—period.

You may be aware that according to the grammatical form in the original language for this passage, the verb "sin" can be translated as "keep on sinning" or "continue to sin" or "make a practice of sinning." So let me give you my own free translation of verse 9: *Whoever is born of God never, ever again, continually practices sin.*

GOD'S SEED WITHIN US

And *why* does the person born of God no longer practice sin continually? John gives us the reason:

Whoever has been born of God does not sin, for His

seed remains in him; and he cannot sin, because he has
been born of God. (1 John 3:9)

Those who have been born by the Spirit of God do not
continually practice sin because God has placed within you
His seed—His Son, and everything about Him. His Son, who
dealt radically with sin on the cross, now dwells within you and
seeks to live out *His* life in *yours*. Christ living within us now
orchestrates our lives to walk free from sin.

One thing we know for sure about the Son of God is that He
has no sin. "In Him there is no sin" (1 John 3:5); He is "without
sin" (Hebrews 4:15); He "knew no sin" (2 Corinthians 5:21);
He is "separate from sinners" (Hebrews 7:26). And now that
the Son of God has taken up residence
within you, shouldn't that make a
difference in regard to sin in your life?
Don't you think His presence would
make you more aware of the danger
of sin, of the consequences of sin, and
of how sin breaks your relationship
with God?

*In the core of your being,
God has placed His provision
for you to live as free
from sin as possible.*

The full meaning of the cross includes the truth that God
has placed a wonderful provision right in the core of your being:
It is the ability to live as free from sin as possible.

"Oh, but Henry," you respond, "we *do* sin."

But what are you doing when you respond in that way?
You're making your own experience the starting point, and
interpreting the Bible by that experience. Instead, you ought
to be lifting your experience to the level of the Word of God.

Why? Because when it comes to sin, God intends for the cross to make a radical difference in your life.

FROM ACTIVE SIN TO ACTIVE RIGHTEOUSNESS

John makes clear in this passage—just as Paul's letters do—that for the true child of God, the active practice of sin is replaced by the active practice of righteousness. The one who keeps sinning is of the devil, but "he who practices righteousness is righteous, just as He [Christ] is righteous" (1 John 3:7). And John adds,

> In this the children of God and the children of the devil are manifest: Whoever does not practice righteousness is not of God, nor is he who does not love his brother. (3:10)

This closely follows what Paul cites as the result of God having made Christ "to be sin for us": In Christ, you and I actually "become the righteousness of God" (2 Corinthians 5:21). We become His righteousness not just in our position before God, but increasingly in the experience of our daily life as well. In the Scriptures, freedom from sin is always connected inseparably with the active pursuit and observance of righteousness.

Does that mean we live a perfect life? Does it mean you're completely free from committing any sin? No, but it does mean a consistent pursuit of holiness and consistent growth in holiness. Though we still commit occasional sins, we no longer *continue* in sin; we no longer *remain* in sin. For the person who's truly born again, staying in sin is an impossibility. Remember again John's words: "No one born of God makes a practice of sinning, for God's seed abides in him, and he *cannot keep on sinning* because he has been born of God" (1 John 3:9, ESV).

THE HOLY SPIRIT AND OUR SIN

The Scriptures tell us that one of the key roles of the Holy Spirit in our lives is to convict us of sin (John 16:8). Aren't you grateful that the Spirit does this? You may think, *Well, I get kind of upset when He does.* But the Spirit helps us get back to reality; it's as if He's saying to us, "Do you know what the cross is all about? Your sin! That's why the cross happened."

Convicting you of sin is the particular and ongoing assignment of the Holy Spirit (John 16:8–11). In view of this, a person who claims to be a Christian but deliberately holds on to a particular sin in his or her life is either totally quenching the Holy Spirit—which is an even worse sin—or has never known the experience of the Holy Spirit's conviction of sin, and isn't a believer at all.

There's no such thing as a genuine child of God who isn't indwelt with the Holy Spirit. God the Father has assigned the Holy Spirit to make absolutely certain that He constantly convicts you of sin, because sin is your ruin. Sin holds back everything God has in mind for you.

When the Holy Spirit convicts a genuine believer of sin, that person can repent and be immediately restored to fellowship with God. But what happens if a Christian doesn't repent? Disaster. That person's heart grows hard, and God's

Word loses its power and fruitfulness in his life. You can always assess your relationship to God by your degree of responsiveness to His Word. For Jesus tells us, "It has been given to you to know the mysteries of the kingdom of heaven"; and He says, "Blessed are your eyes for they see, and your ears for they hear" (Matthew 13:11, 16).

What happens if a Christian doesn't repent? Disaster.

EXCHANGING OUR SIN FOR CHRIST'S RIGHTEOUSNESS

Romans 6 is probably the best chapter in Scripture to help us to know very simply what effect the cross is to have on the Christian's life. I want you to catch the flow of it, because over and over again Paul expresses here the core truth he wants us to know about this—the exchange of our sin for Christ's righteousness.

When God raised up Jesus from the dead, he also brought Christ's life to *you*. His life now becomes your life; the unbounded joy and power of His resurrection are now yours through your union with Him.

I've gone through this chapter hundreds of times, yet as I continue studying it I feel like I'm a child just beginning. The depths of this chapter—both in what it reveals about sin and what it reveals about righteousness—are astounding, and they overwhelm me.

Sometimes people say they have difficulty grasping this passage. I wonder. Could it be that our difficulty in understanding Romans 6 is linked to the fact that we simply aren't *practicing* Romans 6? We prefer to tell ourselves that the sins we indulge in are okay.

MORE SIN FOR MORE GRACE?

Near the end of Romans 5, Paul had stated, "Where sin abounded, grace abounded much more" (5:20). Romans 6 then begins with this question: "What shall we say then? Shall we continue in sin that grace may abound?"

In other words, if grace overflows where sin overflows, why don't we go off and sin all we want? If we want a whole lot of grace, then shouldn't we do a whole lot of sinning?

You may laugh at that reasoning, but that's the way too many Christians live their lives. They tell themselves, "It doesn't matter what I've done, it doesn't matter how far I stray; thank God His grace covers it all!"

What blasphemy! And it's exactly what Paul quickly condemns in Romans 6. He answers his question in the strongest terms: "God forbid! How can we who have died to sin ever live in it again?"

Should Christians feel free not to be overly concerned about lingering sin? The answer is, Impossible! The very nature of our salvation means that God is working in our lives to eradicate our sin. He places within us a horror of sin, because the soul which keeps on sinning will die, and such deadly sin is horrendous to God. He places within us a resolve to do everything to oppose sin and move against any attempt of sin to gain a stronghold in our lives.

If you're a true Christian, indifference toward personal sin is a spiritual impossibility. To maintain such an attitude, you have to move against the activity of the Father, revealing to you the nature of that sin in His Word. You would have to move against the Son, who shows you with His hands and His side what it cost Him. And you would have to move against the Holy Spirit within you, whose job is to convince and convict you of sin.

A true Christian flees sin with a horror.

A true Christian doesn't continue in sin that grace may abound. With the cross ever before him, he flees sin with a horror.

DEATH TO OUR SLAVERY

Paul goes on to describe how we're immersed not only into the death and burial of Christ, but also into His resurrection. God unites us with the whole work of His Son—His crucifixion, burial, death, resurrection, ascension, and His future rule and reign. We enter into a union with Christ Jesus so that the whole process of the cross becomes real in our lives—with this result "that we should *no longer be slaves of sin*" (Romans 6:6).

Slavery to sin was once our inescapable condition. Paul says to all of us, "You were slaves of sin" (Romans 6:17). He reminds each of us of how "you presented your members as slaves of uncleanness, and of lawlessness leading to more lawlessness" (6:19). It was an endlessly downward spiral.

When sin is your master, you have to respond to it. You have to obey; a slave has no other option. When you're the slave of sin and sin gives a command, you submit and comply.

Now, however, that slavery is ended in the cross, as Paul tells us: "But now that you have been set free from sin and have become slaves of God, the fruit you get leads to sanctification and its end, eternal life" (Romans 6:22, ESV).

The death and resurrection of Christ have broken the chains of the sin nature's bondage and control over your life. You're now free to present your body and all that you are unto God.

Ending that bondage requires nothing less than death. In this case, the death of a slave. A dead slave no longer obeys his master; that master can beat his slave's body all he wants, but he'll get no more obedience out of him. At the point of death, an enslaved person finally becomes totally free *not* to respond to his master's call.

That's the picture to keep in mind as we hear Paul say, "Our old man was crucified with Him [with Jesus Christ], that the body of sin might be done away with, that we should no longer be slaves of sin. For *he who has died has been freed from sin*" (Romans 6:6–7). So you are dead to sin. Sin is no longer your master. You don't have to respond anymore when sin tries to command you. In the cross, God dealt with the whole root system of sin so that sin's power over you has been totally broken.

You never again *have* to sin.

This is so profound! You *don't* have to sin; you now have the full power to choose what you'll do.

For example, you have power to decide not to look at pornography, an addiction to so many. In my pastoring over the years, I've learned that pornography is one of the most gripping addictions, and one that can't be broken without the power of

God. Some of the most intense brokenness in confession of sin that I've witnessed from believers has had to do with the sin of pornography, in particular among missionaries and pastors and church leaders.

Do you have the power in your own life over pornography? Yes you do, if you're a genuine believer in Christ. You no longer have any obligation or compulsion or necessity of any kind to serve sin.

Because we died to sin when we opened our life to Christ and acknowledged that our sin crucified Him, we therefore have forever died to sin as our master. We never again have to let sin rule over us. Knowing that our sin crucified the Son of God, how could we possibly continue in sin?

YOUR CHOICE

Paul makes clear the freedom of choice that now is yours.

It's your free choice to "reckon yourselves to be dead indeed to sin, but alive to God in Christ Jesus our Lord" (v. 11).

You're free to choose to "not let sin reign in your mortal body, that you should obey it in its lusts" (v. 12).

You're free to "present yourselves to God as being alive from the dead" (v. 13).

Rather than yielding the parts of your body to sin's control "as instruments of unrighteousness," you're free to offer them to God "as instruments of righteousness to God" (v. 13).

You're free to choose the righteousness that's for the purpose of holiness; though once a slave to sin, you now are "free in regard to righteousness" (vv. 19–20). Now you're unlimited in your capacity to present to God everything you do and everything you are, all for *righteousness*.

So let me ask you: Is there anything in your life that doesn't look like righteousness?

RADICAL NEWNESS

Paul says in Romans 6 that you and I are "set free from sin."

How were we set free? By the cross of Christ. You're set free so that you never again need to respond when sin calls. God has thoroughly defeated sin and Satan, so that when our enemy beckons, we need never tremble. The issue was settled when Christ died, when He dealt with sin and set you free. In your relationship to Christ, all the fullness of God is on the inside of you, causing you to present your bodies to God as instruments of righteousness.

Is there anything in your life that doesn't look like righteousness?

What difference does the cross make? All the difference in the world! It's a difference so radical, so real, so life-transforming, that the only way Paul could put it into words was by calling it *a new creation*.

Remember again those profound words we looked at earlier: "Therefore, if anyone is in Christ, he is a new creation; old things have passed away; behold, all things have become new" (2 Corinthians 5:17). Does this apply only to *some* believers? No, the verse says, *"anyone"*—if *anyone* enters into a relationship with Jesus Christ, God does something radical in you, and He doesn't do it figuratively, but genuinely, personally, and intimately.

How many of those who enter into a saving relationship with Christ have this change in their life? *Every solitary one!* It isn't negotiable; it isn't an option to consider, but a reality to accept and apply and live by. You become immersed into a relationship with Christ so that you're a new creation, with old things passed away and all things becoming new.

Is that hard to understand?

Many of us would have to answer yes. We don't sense "old things passed away" in our lives. We don't sense that "all things have become so new," to the point that we could legitimately be called a new creation.

But here again I must exhort you: *Don't interpret the Scriptures by your experience; interpret your experience by the Word of God!* Raise your experience to the level of what God promises.

WHEN SIN CALLS

Satan, our lying and deceitful adversary will tell you, "Come on! You know you sin. You're a sinner. That's what you do. That's what you are. You're going to keep right on sinning."

How do you deal with that mocking, sneering voice? You won't be able to fight it if you are relying on your personal experience to interpret and determine the meaning of Scripture. The only way to deal with it is to take the truth of Scripture and lay it *over* your experience. Bring your experience up to the Word of God! Let your heart cry out, "God's Word says that I'm never again in bondage to sin, and I don't have to sin. So I come again to my Savior to get victory as I present my body as an instrument of righteousness unto God. I can cover over sin with love. I can take those Scriptures and live them out. I now place my full trust in the Holy Spirit to keep me free by the Word of God and the Truth of God."

So when sin calls, you say no.

The flesh within you will keep resisting righteousness, especially in trying circumstances. When others frustrate you, for example, the flesh within you will insist, "You have a right to be angry!"

But you remind yourself that such anger is not the fruit of the Spirit, but a product of the flesh; the fruit of the Spirit is patience, long-suffering. You know the Scriptures: "Therefore, as the elect of God, holy and beloved, put on tender mercies, kindness, humility, meekness, longsuffering; bearing with one another, and forgiving one another, if anyone has a complaint against another; even as Christ forgave you, so you also must do" (Colossians 3:12–13).

You tell yourself, "I don't have a right to be angry."

So you tell yourself, "I *don't* have a right to be angry."

Your flesh counters, "But don't you see what they've done to you?"

You answer, "Oh, don't you know what they did to the Savior? And He responded to all of it without sin."

As long as we are in this earthly body, sin will seek to make inroads in our lives. If we're not vigilant, if we're not walking in the Spirit, we will give in, making excuses for ourselves.

It's this sinful culture I live in.

It's the way I was brought up.

It's the circumstances I've been through.

It's because I'm so tired.

When sin knocks on your door, reject every excuse that comes to mind! Instead, remember that you belong to Him, body and soul, and keep offering yourself to Him hour by hour, moment by moment.

CHOOSING FREEDOM

Freedom from the clutches of sin has been won for us at great price on the cross. But you still have to choose. Through the death of Jesus Christ on the cross, He broke the power of sin in your life, and you never again have to live under its dominion. You take God at His word and let Him do it. You immediately, this very moment, present your body to God as an instrument of righteousness.

My prayer, with all my heart, is that you would experience the freedom Jesus promised: "If you abide in My word, you are My disciples indeed. And you shall know the truth, and the truth shall make you free" (John 8:31–32).

Is there any area of your life where you sense that you are not absolutely free from sin? If that is true, then release this area—and all of your life—to the truth of God. Ask Him to help you understand His truth and live it out. As you do, your life will become a powerful demonstration of what God did on the cross to deal with sin. The whole world will know by the way you live that sin no longer has dominion over you, and that you are free—totally, joyfully, completely free—in Christ.

CHAPTER 16

THE PATH OF SURRENDER

Free to Fulfill God's Purposes

He who loses his life for My sake will find it.

MATTHEW 10:39

The African nation of Liberia has known great turmoil and bloodshed in recent years. In the aftermath of a particularly bloody period, I visited the country and taught at a ministry retreat there.

A number of missionaries had been shaken and distressed by the violence. One single woman, a veteran of years of service, came to me in tears. "I have a feeling it's time for me to go back and be closer to my relatives," she told me. "My little nieces and nephews don't even know me. I just feel I need to go home."

I asked her to wait on making that decision until our teaching time was over, for we were looking in the Scriptures at many of the things you and I have explored in this book.

SHARING IN CHRIST'S SUFFERINGS

When the retreat ended, she came to me and said, "Henry, God won't let me go home." She mentioned the flood of Liberian refugees who had escaped across the country's borders, leaving countless families torn apart, and she said God assured her of His presence among them. This is the way she put it: "God told me that He was going to go and find them—and He wanted me to go with Him. So I told Him I would go."

While I was there I also met an older missionary who told me how he and his wife had been captured by rebels in the north of Liberia. The rebels imprisoned them in a small room where his wife nearly died. "I've been thinking about everything," this man told me, "and I just think we need to go home."

Later while I was there, this couple came to me and spoke of their renewed assurance of God's love for the rebels, and of hearing God's invitation to go out and take His love to Liberia's scattered people. "So we're going to go," they told me; "it isn't time to return home."

Later I spoke with another missionary who had been in northern Liberia, where the rebels caught and beat him and stole his vehicle and his belongings. The beating brought him lasting physical suffering, but when I asked him to tell me about this, he answered, "I counted the cost before I ever went to Liberia. I told Him ahead of time that I knew the dangers, but as long as He went with me, that was enough." He expressed his gratefulness that though so many others had been killed, his life was spared.

I asked if he resented the treatment he'd received at the hand of the rebels. "Oh, no," he answered. "They treated my

Lord that way." I was reminded again of our Savior's words in Matthew 10:24—"A disciple is not above his teacher, nor a servant above his master."

RELEASED FOR ANYTHING ON GOD'S HEART

I've found that when believers truly understand the cross, it releases them for anything and everything that's on the mind and heart of God in His purpose for them, regardless of the cost. As a result, certain things are no longer an issue for these individuals, things like their willingness to be involved in ministry or on the mission field.

"It isn't time to return home."

Grasping the cross means that missionary work or ministry of any kind becomes an incredible privilege, granted to you by the God who saved you so you could live out your life for Him. When you comprehend the cross you no longer have to wrestle with "Would I be willing to go and live in Africa?" You realize that the distance between your comfortable home now and Africa is infinitely small compared to the distance for Christ between the shining glory of God's throne in heaven and the darkness of His death on the cross.

How do you even measure the difference and the distance between the glory of God's heaven and the dark depths of the cross of Calvary?

It's beyond measure.

So how could we ever worry or fuss about going to Africa,

if He in His perfect love and knowledge asks us to go? Paul says, "The love of Christ compels us" (2 Corinthians 5:14)— the love of Christ makes the decision for us. But we have to fill that love full of meaning through our active obedience.

Are you letting His love compel your actions and decisions? Or do you find yourself (by your actions) saying to God, "Not Your will, but mine be done."

THE CROSS AND THE COST

On the cross, Jesus surrendered Himself completely to the will of the Father.

And that's what the cross means for you and me, too. It's about a cost we have to pay because of the cost that Jesus had to pay.

And He says that unless we pay this cost, we aren't even worthy to follow Him—"He who does not take his cross and follow after Me is not worthy of Me" (Matthew 10:38).

Have you counted the cost?

Some years ago on a visit to Indonesia, I spoke with a missionary who told me about an Indonesian pastor she knew who lived in a mountainous area on the coast of Java. This man knew some English and had been part of a study group going through the workbook *Experiencing God,* which had a tremendous impact on his life. Now he greatly desired his own people to also go through *Experiencing God,* and to gain the same benefit and joy he had derived from the book. As a result, he had begun translating the book into his people's native language, working for a few hours every day at a manual typewriter.

But the real uniqueness of this story, as the missionary explained it to me, was that this man was a leper.

I knew something about leprosy. I knew that lepers often lose part of their fingers, and also that they cannot sit still long. So an image came immediately to my mind of how much this dear pastor must be suffering so his people could experience more of the love of God.

I asked the missionary, "Will you be seeing this man again?"

"Yes," she said.

I said, "Would you let him know that the coauthor of *Experiencing God* would like to ask a favor from him? Would you ask if he would let you take his picture sitting at his manual typewriter with his fingers on the keys and with his papers and the book *Experiencing God* there before him? And let him know that the reason I want this picture is so it will help me pray for him in his work."

The missionary replied that the pastor was a modest and humble man, and she didn't know whether he would agree to my request. "But I'll ask him," she said.

About two years later I was at a church convention and heard a voice calling my name. I turned and saw this missionary approaching me, and she was calling out, "I got it! I got it!"

Of course, by that time I'd forgotten my request. "Great," I told her. "What did you get?"

She said, "I got the picture!" And she showed it to me. Now I have it framed in a little prayer room off the side of my office, and it reminds me of the willingness of a child of God to bear any cost to be a part of God's will and the ministry of His love to those around Him.

YOUR CROSS MUST BE CHOSEN

This Indonesian pastor might have decided that his leprosy was already enough difficulty for one life, and he didn't need to bother about sacrificing to serve others according to God's will. But he saw the truth more clearly.

I've had many a person describe a physical handicap to me and then say, "That's my cross." But a cross isn't something that you *have* to bear—something you have no choice about. It's something that you *choose* to bear.

When Jesus tells you to take up your cross, He isn't talking about simply resigning yourself to unavoidable circumstances, to some physical handicap you can't avoid and have no choice about. He's calling you instead to a dynamic choice you must make about the Father's will and His ways. These things will only be a part of your life if you choose them in obedience.

THE CROSS AND THE WILL OF GOD

When Jesus talked to His disciples about taking up the cross and following Him, did He have a specific meaning in mind for that word *cross?* Yes, Jesus understood thoroughly what He had in mind. Did He mean a real cross? Yes, He meant a real cross. And His disciples were going to witness that very graphically.

You'll recall our earlier exploration of the divine necessity of the cross. This necessity is reflected in a certain small word that occurs repeatedly in the teachings of Jesus about His suffering.

He spoke this little word as He foretold His disciples what would happen to Him: "Jesus began to show to His disciples that He *must* go to Jerusalem, and suffer many things from the elders and chief priests and scribes, and be killed, and be raised the third day" (Matthew 16:21).

He used it as well on the evening in the Upper Room when He shared the Passover meal with His disciples: "I say to you that this which is written *must* still be accomplished in Me: 'And He was numbered with the transgressors'" (Luke 22:37).

A cross isn't something you have to bear— it's something you choose to bear.

Later that same night, in the tense moment of His arrest, Jesus used this little word again: "It *must* happen thus" (Matthew 26:54); "The Scriptures *must* be fulfilled" (Mark 14:49).

And He used it again after His resurrection, as He continued teaching His disciples: "All things *must* be fulfilled which were written in the Law of Moses and the Prophets and the Psalms concerning Me" (Luke 24:44).

To the Lord Jesus, the cross was very real and the divine necessity of it was very real—and all of it was unbreakably linked with the simple matter of doing His Father's will. He knew the Father's will included the cross, so He always kept moving in that direction.

When you look at the life of the Lord Jesus and see how He handles the Father's will, you're also seeing how He handles the Father's will in *your* life as well. How could it be otherwise? Isn't it a fact that He is living out His life in you?

Jesus said, "I have come down from heaven, not to do My own will, but the will of Him who sent Me" (John 6:38). That's the same reason He has come down from heaven to dwell in your life. Doing the Father's will was and is a constant for Him. He knows the will of God for your life, and knows it thoroughly. And as you surrender the days and hours of your life to Him, He's living it out.

Our Cross and God's Will for Us

When we talk about the cross in the Christian's life, we're talking about releasing your life in such a way that Christ can express Himself in you and through you.

Paul says in Philippians 2:5, "Let this mind be in you which was also in Christ Jesus." That word *let* tells us that Paul is speaking of a choice—something we can let happen or not.

Then Paul shows us this mind of Christ which we can allow to be our own mindset as well. He tells us how Jesus…

…though he was in the form of God, did not count equality with God a thing to be grasped, but made himself nothing, taking the form of a servant, being born in the likeness of men. And being found in human form, he humbled himself by becoming obedient to the point of death, even death on a cross. (Philippians 2:6–8, ESV)

Though He was God, Christ didn't cling to His rights, but gave them over to the Father. So when Paul tells us to have this same mind that Christ had, he's telling us to let God have His way to accomplish His purpose in our life, even to death on a cross—no matter what it costs.

The cross represented the will of God for Jesus. In the same way, the cross for you is the will of God that He desires to work out in your life, whatever that may involve. *Your cross is whatever God reveals as His personal will for you.*

The cross for Jesus was that ultimate purpose of God to bring salvation to our world; the cross in your life will be a choice to turn over everything in your life to God, to let God's ultimate purpose come to pass in your life, whatever this requires from you. For every believer, the cross is the sign and symbol for obediently carrying out the will of God.

The cross for you is the will of God that He desires to work out in your life.

As Paul reasoned with the Philippians about the believer's commitment to the will of God, he wrote:

> Therefore, my beloved, as you have always obeyed, not as in my presence only, but now much more in my absence, work out your own salvation with fear and trembling; for it is God who works in you both to will and to do for His good pleasure. (Philippians 2:12–13)

Let me reword that. Paul is saying, "Let the greatness of God's salvation work itself into every solitary corner of your life, and do it with fear and trembling, because God is working in you both to will and to do for His good pleasure."

Christ, knowing the will of the Father, released His life to the Father's will. He allowed His Father to work in every corner of His life, knowing that the result would be a great salvation for all humanity. In the same way, we can trust God to show His greatness through our obedience as well. If you walk in right relationship to God, He will bring to completion His amazing will for your life, and nothing in your circumstances can ultimately thwart that.

Trusting God's Perfect Knowledge and Love

I think the greatest thing God did for me in my childhood was to convince me beyond any question or doubt that He was God and I was not. In the years since then, I've never approached God any other way. It doesn't cross my mind to question Him, since I know His way is best and I want to always adapt my ways to His. He knows everything about my tomorrows, and His perfect love can never give me second best.

This was proven for all time when He gave His Son for me:

> God is love. In this the love of God was manifested toward us, that God has sent His only begotten Son into the world, that we might live through Him. In this is love, not that we loved God, but that He loved us and sent His Son to be the propitiation for our sins. (1 John 4:8–10)

This is why every directive God gives for your life or mine

is another expression of His perfect love for the entire world. But it even goes beyond that, stretching the limits of our finite minds: He leads us in His will with perfect knowledge of every factor and circumstance in the past, present, and future, and on into all of eternity. And every directive God gives is always accompanied by His presence and power to enable us to accomplish and carry out His will.

So why discuss it? Why even think of arguing with Him or complaining? Would we want any *less* than God can give? What could be more unwise than that?

That's why the way in which you respond to God's directives always demonstrates what you truly believe about Him—about His wisdom and His love. And what you believe about God will always come into deeper truth and clearer focus as you grow in your sustained understanding of the cross. What you're doing at this moment in your relationship to God is the clearest indication of what you truly believe about Him, regardless of any verbal claim you might make. You may say, "Lord, I just want You to know what's on my heart"—and He does. David poured out his heart before the Lord again and again in the psalms. He is your Father, and He delights to hear your voice.

But ultimately, the key to your life is not what's on your heart, but what's on *His* heart.

OBEDIENCE IS OBEDIENCE

Once we know God's guidelines, then our response—whatever we do next—is either sin or righteousness. Either we follow what He says or not.

Sometimes believers will shrink from what God asks them to do because the standard seems too high. "After all," they say, "nobody's perfect." But He challenges us on that: "In other words, you're planning to be disobedient. You're planning *not* to obey, simply because you don't think you can."

God never accepts our excuses when we try to justify why we aren't doing what He tells us. Obedience is obedience, and anything less than obedience is disobedience.

Some will say, "But, Lord, I've tried."

And God answers, "I didn't tell you to try. I told you to *do it.*"

You may say, "Lord, I sense what You're telling me to do, but You just need to know I'm having trouble with that." He will answer, "What you're saying, My child, is that you really don't love and trust Me. If you believe correctly, you'll respond correctly—in unquestioned obedience."

You cannot have your will and His will at the same time.

It comes down to this: Would you rather follow your own best thinking for your life, or God's best purposes? And you cannot begin to grasp the incredible purposes of God unless you learn to see them in the right context—that is, unless you view everything in the light of eternity and in the light of God's eternal plan of redemption.

THE DIFFICULTY OF SELF-DENIAL

Every disciple of Christ needs to be made aware that in following Christ, there are certain things that come first before other things. We so often want to skip the cross and go straight to Pentecost—to avoid the suffering and go straight to spiritual power and testimony and impact. But the cross must come first. Denying of self comes first. Before you can experience more of the wonders that come following Him, you must deny self and take up your cross.

I've often had people say to me how difficult it is for them to deny self. All of us have that difficulty, don't we?

But let me tell you what I do in facing that difficulty. When I know of something He requires of me that's particularly hard to implement in my life, I come quietly before the Lord and say, "Lord, I know this is what You require, yet I'm finding it difficult for me. But if You will enable me and work in me and show me how to do this, I'll respond to You immediately."

We so often want to skip the cross and go straight to Pentecost.

The moment you acknowledge your need and come to Him seeking His provision and releasing your life for Him to work, He'll show you what it means to deny self. You'll see it very radically, and you'll see it very thoroughly. So be willing to respond to any requirement He may ask, and you'll know the experience of God Himself helping you. You'll see how He never fails to do what He promised to do. He who began a good work in you will complete it—that's an absolute with God. But don't expect this path to be a popular one with everyone around you.

ONLY BY THE NARROW WAY

Do you remember in the Gospels the critical factor of *narrowness* that Jesus taught His disciples about? He said, "Strive to enter through the narrow gate" (Luke 13:24). He said, "Narrow is the gate and difficult is the way which leads to life, and there are few who find it" (Matthew 7:14).

If you think deeply about those words, you may hear Jesus saying, "There's a way that leads to true, vibrant life—in your marriage, in your family, in your church, in your workplace. But it's not the path the majority takes, and the entrance to it is very restricted. It's not the way most believers are walking, and that's why there's so little victory, so little experience of the power of the cross and the power of the resurrection."

Hearing this challenge, we need to cry out to the Lord with great earnestness of heart: "O God, don't let me miss it! Don't let me assume I'm taking the narrow and difficult way when in fact I'm on the same wide path as everyone else."

The majority are simply not interested in the narrow gate and the difficult path.

The majority are simply not interested in the narrow gate and the difficult path. It's very true in the practice of prayer, for example. Very few want to walk the restricted way of the Scripture that says, "The effective, fervent prayer of a righteous man avails much" (James 5:16). When you set your feet on that pathway of prayer—earnest, agonizing prayer—you look around for companions and they'll not be there. Very, very few of God's people ever walk that path.

If you want to have the fullest impact of the cross in your life, don't be surprised to discover there are few who want to walk that road with you. But don't be discouraged. That fact ought to be confirmation that you're taking the narrow way. If you look to God instead of to people, He'll affirm for you that you're on the right track. And it may be that God intends to use the witness of your walk on the narrow way to bring His presence and power to many others around you.

THE DOORS HE SOMETIMES CLOSES

Listen carefully to what Jesus went on to say after talking about the narrow gate:

> Strive to enter through the narrow gate, for many, I say to you, will seek to enter and will not be able. When once the Master of the house has risen up and shut the door, and you begin to stand outside and knock at the door, saying, "Lord, Lord, open for us," and He will answer and say to you, "I do not know you, where you are from," then you will begin to say, "We ate and drank in Your presence, and You taught in our streets." But He will say, "I tell you I do not know you, where you are from. Depart from Me, all you workers of iniquity." (Luke 13:24–27)

Many believers somehow have the idea that any time they ask God to open the door, He'll say at once, "I'm so glad you asked; come on in!" But that isn't true. There are those who will want to get in where Christ is, where the power of the cross is, where the power of the resurrection is, and He will answer "Depart from Me. *I have never known you.*"

It's not a matter of whether you *say* you know Him. Don't you suppose there were many in Jesus' day who eagerly heard Him teach, who gladly saw His miracles, and who would easily testify that they knew Him? They would say, "Oh, yes, I know Jesus." But would He necessarily say that *He* knew *them?* No, not necessarily. To be around Him and to observe Him is not the same as having an intimate relationship with Him, of truly knowing one another.

The key to your life is not whether you can say you know Him, but whether *He* can say to you, "I know you." And that's a whole different ball game.

The Savior's words about the narrow gate are found also in Matthew 7:13–14, and soon afterward comes this exceedingly painful passage:

Not everyone who says to Me, "Lord, Lord," shall enter the kingdom of heaven, but he who does the will of My Father in heaven. Many will say to Me in that day, "Lord, Lord, have we not prophesied in Your name, cast out demons in Your name, and done many wonders in Your name?" And then I will declare to them, "I never knew you; depart from Me, you who practice lawlessness!" (Matthew 7:21–23)

So it doesn't matter if a person can say he knows Jesus. After all, the demons know Him, do they not? They knew Him even before He came to earth. And seeing Him come to earth, they know He lived a sinless life, that He died for the sins of the world, that God raised Him up the third day in victory over sin, that He now sits at the right hand of the Father interceding for us, and that He's coming back again. The demons know all that. So what's the difference between them and a Christian?

The Christian is one who chooses to release His life unconditionally to Jesus' right to be Lord. The Christian no longer lives to self, but unto Him who died for us and was raised again. The true Christian does what Jesus said. The true Christian denies self—that is, cancels self, knowing that self is the source of all of our disconnection with God—and takes up a cross, and follows Him.

And those who do this are few.

Will you be one of the few who says to the Lord, "Not my will, but Thine be done"? Let the Spirit of God bring to your heart an understanding of what this looks like in your life, and all that it will involve.

CHAPTER 17

THE PATH OF DISCIPLESHIP

How to Finish Strong

*A disciple is not above his teacher,
nor a servant above his master.*

MATTHEW 10:24

I passed my seventieth birthday not long ago, and it was a good time to look back on decade after decade of witnessing and experiencing God's continuing faithfulness. I see the present time for me as a season when God is gathering up everything He's ever done in my life, bringing it all together into a tighter focus. I'm always looking at my present opportunities and circumstances, and seeing how this relates to where God has brought me in the past and to what I sense He's calling me to in the future.

I can see how God is building on every moment in my past where He helped me to be faithful, and He's using that as a platform from which I can continue to speak to others everywhere. By His grace I've been given unusual opportunities that very few are given to bring the Lord's Word into certain places, and the awareness of this privilege and this calling causes me to tremble before every opportunity to speak, and before every assignment I receive from God.

I'm praying for good health for this, because the schedule and the travel are demanding. When people ask, "How can I pray for you?" I often mention my health as well as two other things: I ask them to pray that I'll always have the message God wants for these particular people to hear, and second, that I can share that message in a way that even a ten-year-old can understand it. And I feel very serious about that.

Carelessness and casualness are among the greatest failures of God's people today.

I often say that my wife keeps me humble and my five children and fourteen grandchildren keep me poor. So I'm both poor and humble by God's divine purpose, and I rest in that blessing, because I have every reason to be full of joy, after a lifetime spent as a disciple of our Savior and Shepherd.

THE SHEEP AND THE SHEPHERD

The Bible says we're like sheep, and since that's true, is it not important that we keep following our Shepherd faithfully?

Our constant natural tendency is to wander, to grow slack and lose our diligence and discipline and seriousness, and I believe this kind of carelessness and casualness are among the greatest failures of God's people today. We find it so easy to get distracted as we follow the latest fads or the latest celebrities or the latest events, and forget to follow the Shepherd. We forget that to be a friend of the world is to be an enemy of God (James 4:4). Does that grieve the heart of the Father? Yes it does.

But what pleases the heart of the Father is when we can truly say with Paul that our only boast in life is "the cross of our Lord Jesus Christ, by whom the world has been crucified to me, and I to the world" (Galatians 6:14). The cross shows us how to die to the world's hold upon us, and it opens up our understanding for walking the path of discipleship, for a lifetime of following our Savior and Shepherd.

Remember again the words Jesus spoke in Luke 14:27: "Whoever does not bear his cross and come after Me cannot be My disciple." He didn't say you won't be a very good disciple or a particularly effective disciple, but rather that you cannot even *be* His disciple apart from bearing your cross.

Without the cross, there is no discipleship. And in this chapter I want to touch on a few significant matters for every disciple who follows the Lord in the way of the cross.

A DISCIPLE MAINTAINS AN ETERNAL PERSPECTIVE

I've often thought about the importance of our capacity, as believers in Christ, to see more than what the world sees.

Near the end of her life, Helen Keller said that even with her blindness and deafness, she believed she had come to know and experience more of Christ than the average Christian ever did. Though deaf and blind, she came to hear the voice of God and to see the acts and the character of God in profound ways.

The world says that seeing is believing; but God says that believing is seeing. When you have the eyes of faith, you see more than physical eyes can ever see, because you can perceive the eternity we were created for.

God didn't create us for time; He created us for eternity. Time is simply our opportunity to get to know Him and prepare for the eternity He created us for, the eternity which is also the ultimate reason for the cross.

But we seldom think in those terms. As a matter of fact, I think the average Christian has developed little capacity to think about eternity. So we don't know how to effectively respond when we read a scripture such as this word from Jesus in the Sermon on the Mount: "Lay up for yourselves treasures in heaven" (Matthew 6:20).

Paul said that if our hope in Christ is for this life alone, then Christians are the most pitiable of all people (1 Corinthians 15:19). If all we get is in this life, is it really worth it? But God in His Word assures us that this world is not what life's all about.

A DISCIPLE JOYFULLY ENDURES

The way of the cross means a lifetime of perseverance and endurance, but I want to emphasize that if knowing this only makes you grim and joyless, you're missing a very important part of the truth of the cross.

The Scriptures tell us that Jesus endured the cross "for the *joy* that was set before Him" (Hebrews 12:2). The joy He looked forward to, the hope that He knew, the confident expectation He experienced—this is available for every believer, and it allows us to endure whatever the cross will mean for us in self-denial and suffering by the will of God.

Yes, there is a cross for us—but that doesn't cancel the joy. There's always a resurrection beyond the cross, and this is what makes it worth it all after you've been faithful to bear the cost and to endure.

Marilynn and I have lived long enough to be able to bear witness of many moments in our lives together

Yes, there is a cross—but that doesn't cancel the joy.

which could be described as a cross. But they were not the end.

If you focus exclusively on the cross you're bearing, and don't see beyond it, you'll never be able to endure that cross well.

The cross is never the end. It's only partway through. The cross is necessary, but the cross is always accompanied by the resurrection, and the victory that comes from the resurrection then explodes upon a watching and waiting world. That's always true.

REMEMBERING GOD'S FORGIVENESS

I've known many who want out when the pain of their cross seems to become unbearable. And let me add that this is often particularly true in regard to the difficulties we face as our children grow older and become involved in serious trouble. I can recall many tearful hours in the middle of the night praying for what I was experiencing with our children.

As others have faced such difficulties, I've heard many describe the indescribable pain of finally coming to a tough-love decision to ask their son or daughter to leave home. My response is to recall a situation with one of my children which was as grievous in its own way as anything I've seen in other families. At that time, I had been receiving an abundance of "tough love" counsel from others.

In the midst of this trial, I was on my face on our living room floor in the middle of the night, and the Lord said to me, "Henry, I had rules in My house, too, and you broke every one of them. But I never kicked you out. I loved you, and I forgave you and forgave you and forgave you." That began a new way of thinking for me on how to deal with the pain that comes from raising children.

There is joy beyond the crosses we bear in raising children, so don't become weary in well doing! What it's costing you in the process will be worth it all when the victory comes after you've been faithful.

THE CROSS IN THE CHURCH FAMILY

The reality of the cross is true not only in our marriages and with our children, but also with local church families.

Church families go through times of pain, and are called to bear a cross together. They're meant to stay together in enduring that cross, rather than having church members depart in search of greener pastures. And I bear witness to you that there's no victory for the people of God in the life of any local church without a cross that's followed by the resurrection.

All three of the churches where I was pastor for a significant amount of time were very broken churches, scarred by division and discouragement. The sin of God's people leaves a pain to endure, but we endured it, and in time the churches thrived. Why did they thrive? Because after the cross, there's power in the resurrection to bring resolution. In the cross of Jesus Christ, we see what sin can do when it does its worst, but resurrection follows the cross, and I'm grateful that I've been able to experience that in the churches I've served.

Most of us want great revival in our churches, we want a Pentecost in our churches, but we want it without the cross. But it can't happen that way. The cross always precedes Pentecost, and the outpouring of God's Spirit and God's power.

The One who has called you to bear your cross will also go with you.

You cannot have the resurrection and the victory without the cross. It's true in our families and in our churches as well as in our individual lives. But you can thank the Father that He's there with you as you endure the cross you bear, and you can commit everything into His hands, knowing that beyond the time of suffering there'll be a resurrection by the power of Almighty God.

There is a cross, but the One who has called you to bear it will also go with you, and He knows how to fulfill the Father's will. If He's taken up residence in your life, will He not be enabling you to do the same thing?

I bear witness that after the Gethsemane there will be a cross, and after the cross there will be a resurrection, and after the resurrection there will be a Pentecost.

A DISCIPLE IS IMMERSED IN GOD'S WORD

The way of a disciple, the way of the cross, always means a continual looking and listening to the Word of God.

We stay with the Word of God so the Spirit of God can open our minds and our hearts to the truth of God, the truth that reveals His ways and His character. If you don't know God and His ways, you can be going totally contrary to Him and not know it. Only by the Word of God can you fully know whether you're living in a way that's in harmony with Him or contrary to Him.

Someone once asked me if I knew a good book to help him in resolving conflicts in the church.

I said, "I do—First and Second Corinthians."

His face dropped, and he said, "That really wasn't what I was asking."

"My brother," I replied, "I knew that wasn't what you were asking. You wanted me to recommend a book by men. But why don't you go back to the textbook God gave us?" Our problem is that we're reading so many human books but neglecting the Bible. But don't ever replace the Bible with a book by men (including the ones I've written). And don't even bother to read other books unless they press you into the Scriptures. In what we face today, we don't need human reasoning; we need divine revelation.

That's why it's critically important that each of us spend quality, quantity time in the Word of God. Never say you're too busy to do it, because that only shows you've simply replaced real life with mere activity. Most of us, when we say we're extremely busy, are talking about activity, not relationship, which is real life. If you continue in the busyness of your life to the exclusion of quality time in the Word of God, it will be disastrous. You cannot experience the fullness of God apart from quality time in the Word of God.

When you read a passage in Scripture, realize that every word there is critically important, and every truth brings you face-to-face with God, not with just a "concept" or "interesting idea." You're face-to-face with who God is and what He does, as He opens your eyes to recognize His activity.

> *All the presence of God is found in every phrase.*

Linger long on every phrase, because all the presence of God is found there. And the longer you meditate, the more the truth will seem to overwhelm you. The shorter the meditation, the quicker you can close your Bible, have a brief prayer, and go on your way. Of course, even the shortest of meditations will benefit your life and strengthen your soul. But you will have missed so much by being in a hurry.

When you meditate, stand in the presence of God and say to Him, in one way or another, "Lord, tell me what You mean by what You're saying here. And tell me how this should affect my own life." When you do that, every verse becomes a whole universe of information and challenge. You stand with an openness before God in the process, and nearly always what you're experiencing in His presence through His Word will apply dramatically to what you're going to be involved in next, according to His will.

So always keep yourself immersed in the Word of God.

A DISCIPLE PRAYS TO DISCERN
GOD'S WILL

> "For I know the thoughts that I think toward you, says
> the LORD, thoughts of peace and not of evil, to give you
> a future and a hope." (Jeremiah 29:11)

Perhaps when you were younger, you memorized this wonderful verse to help you remember God's perspective for the years ahead. But don't stop with verse 11! Remember to take to heart also the words that immediately follow:

> "Then you will call upon Me and go and pray to Me, and
> I will listen to you. And you will seek Me and find Me,
> when you search for Me with all your heart." (29:12–13)

What could be more encouraging than that? What an incentive to pray!

The way of a disciple, the way of the cross, is a pathway of continual prayer, just as Jesus showed us by example. The gospels show us again and again how Jesus prayed so intensely before and during the major transitions in His ministry.

As we saw earlier, Scripture says that "in the days of His flesh" Jesus "offered up prayers and supplications, with vehement cries and tears to Him who was able to save Him from death, and was heard because of His godly fear" (Hebrews 5:7). This intensity of prayer was deeply and profoundly linked with how Jesus lived out His obedience to the will of God, even unto the cross. The passage goes on to say: "Though He was a

Son, yet He learned obedience by the things which He suffered. And having been perfected, He became the author of eternal salvation to all who obey Him" (5:8–9).

We know that in Gethsemane, Jesus fell on His face and prayed, "O My Father, if it is possible, let this cup pass from Me; nevertheless, not as I will, but as You will." And what was God's answer? *No.*

Some Christians say with frustration, "I prayed, but God didn't hear me," when what they mean is, "God didn't do what I told Him to do." But God doesn't intend to do what you tell Him to do. Prayer isn't designed to get God to do our will; prayer is designed so that we can stand in His presence and know what *His* will is, and submit to it.

And whenever God answers no to your prayers, what you believe about God will be quickly revealed in what you do next. What did Jesus do next? He said, "Not My will, but Thine be done." And He rose up from Gethsemane's ground and submitted to His Father's exact will for Him at that moment, which meant arrest, torture, and the cross.

So never lose the connection between the cross, the will of God, and the true purpose of prayer.

CHAPTER 18

THE PATH OF WITNESS AND MINISTRY

Taking His Cross to Your World

> *I am not ashamed of the gospel of Christ, for it is the power of God to salvation for everyone who believes.*

ROMANS 1:16

I once received a phone call from a man wanting help from a pastor. He said he'd already talked with four other pastors, "and three of them said you're the only pastor who works with people like me."

I asked him, "What's your problem?"

"I'm an alcoholic," he answered.

I invited him to come at once to see me, and promised to talk with him and help him until God delivered him from alcohol. I didn't know until later that he was phoning from a downtown hotel where he was standing on the windowsill of an upper floor, and he'd decided that if I said I wouldn't help him, he would jump and end his life.

BEING AN ANSWER TO
SOMEONE'S PRAYER

The process of helping this tortured man continued for many months. There were times when I had to go into town and pull him out of bars—and even out of prostitutes' rooms. But finally the day came when he knelt in the home of one of the deacons in our church and put his faith in Christ. I remember the moment well, and I can still hear his prayer as he cried out unto God.

A few weeks later a small gray-haired lady who I didn't recognize came up to me after church. She was crying as she stepped forward to hug me. I soon discovered that this man I'd been helping was the only one of her children who had walked away from God. This godly mother, who I learned was active in organizing support for missionary efforts, had spent many sleepless nights because of her son, and she told me she would pray for him something like this: "O God, I don't know where my son is, but I love him, and I pray that somehow You'll put some caring Christian alongside of him, someone who'll stay with him long enough until he's saved."

Maybe you've prayed a prayer much like that for someone you know. I know I have. As this mother told me this, I realized how my reaching out to this man had been an answer to her prayer.

Do you realize that around your life today there are probably lost people whose mothers or fathers are praying that God will put a Christian alongside them? And *you* are that person.

HANGING IN THE BALANCE

At that moment in Gethsemane, when the whole eternal purpose of the Father was hanging in the balance, Jesus responded by saying, "Not My will, but Thine be done." God's eternal plan of redemption was carried forward.

And now, what follows for you and me is a moment just as critical, a moment that God has entrusted to each of us.

Not only did He purpose the world's redemption. Not only did He accomplish it in the freely given death of His beloved Son. Not only did He raise His Son, and seat Him at His right hand as an intercessor. Not only did He pour out the Holy Spirit. But He is also resting on you and me the responsibility for the redemption of the entire world.

He is resting on you and me the responsibility for the redemption of the entire world.

The whole purpose of the cross was that all men everywhere would have the opportunity to hear the good news of what God has provided, and we are the bearers of that gospel. He's depending on you and me. The Father waits and all heaven stands silent to see how those who have been redeemed will respond to the request from their Redeemer to take His message to the world. And if we say no, the whole eternal purpose of God for some is never fulfilled.

How do you suppose the Father feels about that? How do you suppose He feels when He has redeemed us at the cost of the cross, only to find us saying, "Not Your will, but mine be done"?

Each of us must decide for ourselves that we will have no part in causing such grief to Him, and that instead we'll further fulfill His plan of redemption by doing our part as His messengers. For if you and I do what He told us to do, then He will do what only He can do in accomplishing His salvation in the lives of those around us. Everyone within your circle of influence, in ever-increasing ways, will feel the impact of what it means for the Lord Jesus Christ to rule in your heart.

MINISTRY OF RECONCILIATION

We've come to the final aspect of the cross that we have room for in this book, and it's this: Not only does God save you, and not only does He claim the right to your life, but He also gives you a particular ministry, as Paul tells us: God "has reconciled us to Himself through Jesus Christ, and has given us the ministry of reconciliation" (2 Corinthians 5:18). God gave you a ministry of reconciliation. Did you fully accept that when you became a Christian?

This gift means that the measure of grace He has extended to you becomes immediately the measure of grace He wants you to extend to all others who need it. That's the true measure of your understanding of God's grace in saving you. Has it become the immediate standard by which you deal with everyone else?

Are there people in your life who you're convinced do not deserve to be dealt with in this gracious way? Probably so. But still God simply says, "The measure to use in your dealings with them is the fact that I did not attribute your sin to you, but instead brought you into perfect harmony with My holiness through the death of My Son. And now you forever have an obligation of extending grace in the same way."

AMBASSADORS FOR CHRIST

Because we have this ministry to others of grace and reconciliation from God, Paul next tells us more of what this means: "Now then, we are ambassadors for Christ, as though God were pleading through us" (2 Corinthians 5:20).

By the very nature of your salvation, you immediately become an ambassador for Jesus Christ. This is the logical, immediate outcome of becoming the "new creation" that Paul speaks of in verse 17, and of being given the "ministry of reconciliation" that he describes in verse 19.

Isn't it amazing that when you're an ambassador for Christ, it's *God Himself* who's pleading through you? All of 2 Corinthians 5 is such an amazing and incredible message, but this is what's especially overwhelming for me: Our life becomes the resident presence of God pleading with those around us to be reconciled to God

Our life becomes the resident presence of God pleading with those around us.

through the death of Jesus Christ, who is God's provision for that reconciliation.

It would be impossible to keep quiet any person who truly understood that. You'd never have to give him a soul-winning study course. You'd never have to teach him how to witness, because he would instinctively *be* a witness. You could no more silence people who have gone through this experience than you could plug Niagara Falls with a paper bag. From within their inmost being, God orchestrates a deep, passionate concern to let the gospel of God go forth and to let His kingdom be expanded. This comes bubbling forth like water from an artesian well.

So our responsibility is to be an ambassador for Christ. This simply means allowing the amazement, gratitude, and boundless joy of our redemption to light up our faces and fill our mouth with the overflow of His goodness in our lives. We will be constantly urging and helping others to understand what God has done—our words bearing the same love and intensity as if God Himself were stating them.

This intensity means that when you're trying to lead others to faith in Christ, you help them fully understand what they're doing. You help them understand the significance of their sin. You help them know that the wages of sin is death, an eternal separation from God, a death which is inevitable if they don't accept God's only provision. And then comes the good news: God, because He loved you and doesn't want you to experience that death, now calls you to repent of your sin, to have faith in what God has done and now offers you through Jesus Christ.

Paul also says in this passage, "The love of Christ compels us" (v. 14). That's why Paul endured all that he endured as a servant of the gospel.

It wasn't "duty" or "guilt" or "obligation" that sent him out, risking his very life, to the frontiers of the civilized world.

It was love.

MINISTRY TO THE WORLD

When Paul said that the world had been crucified to him (Galatians 6:14), he did not mean that he was withdrawing himself from the real world. On the contrary, it enabled him to function profoundly and thoroughly and completely in the real world.

And what helped Paul to function that way? It was His understanding of the cross. In the same verse he said, "Far be it from me to boast except in the cross of our Lord Jesus Christ" (ESV). His encounter and experience of the power of the cross and the wisdom of the cross was so radical in his life that it controlled how he approached the entire world.

No apostle of Jesus was more completely involved than Paul was in the midst of the world, and yet was so totally separated from the world system. He did not think the way the world thought, but he brought the thinking of God to the world, and saw it transformed.

And this of course is exactly what Jesus wants for us.

This is what He prayed so earnestly for us.

Remember the words He spoke to His Father about His disciples? "I do not pray that You should take them out of the world, but that You should keep them from the evil one. They are not of the world, just as I am not of the world.... As You sent Me into the world, I also have sent them into the world" (John 17:15–18).

If there's anything we see in Scripture that seems to be on the heart of God, it is that He loves *the world*, and He does so in a way that effectively counters Satan and the evil world system he controls.

WILL YOU EXERCISE THIS GIFT?

If then, when the Lord God transformed you, He also gave you this ministry of reconciliation to take into your world, are you going to exercise it? Will you allow Him to do this through you? Ultimately you must face this question.

Will you seek to bring your family members into a reconciled relationship to God?

Ultimately you must face this question.

Will you take God's message of reconciliation into your workplace, and earnestly seek God's way to bring His message to the people there—lovingly, without pressure, and without forcing it?

Will you do it with your neighbors and your friends?

Remember that the cross isn't complete unless it includes these things in your life. This is all a part of the full event of the cross, and as it further unfolds, it will look just like this in your life and mine. That's what we'll see of the activity of God. That's what we'll see of the power of the cross, as the eternal plan in the heart and mind of God reaches fulfillment.

FOR A LIFETIME OF STUDY

It has been my privilege to share these truths of the cross with you through these pages. At the start of the book I mentioned that this is an extremely demanding theme, one that makes me tremble. And it's one for which words so often fail; you express these things in the clearest words you can, and yet you still feel that it's so inadequate, that it hasn't been enough.

But I can tell you one thing. The One who is your Teacher, the Holy Spirit, will guide you into all truth. He will teach you all things and He'll bring all things into reality in your life.

May this book have been an introduction on your part to a lifetime of study in the Scriptures on the cross of Christ and its place in the heart and mind of God from eternity. May you clearly see how sin—your sin and mine—is the reason for the cross. May you realize more deeply than ever that in the cross God dealt with our sin so radically and so decisively.

And may you therefore be able to affirm with ever-increasing conviction and understanding, "I have been crucified with Christ, and it is no longer I who live, but Christ lives in me! And the life I now live in the flesh I live by faith in the Son of God, who loved *me* and gave Himself for *me.*"

STEPS TO PEACE WITH GOD

1. RECOGNIZE GOD'S PLAN—PEACE AND LIFE

The message in this book stresses that God loves you and wants you to experience His peace and life.

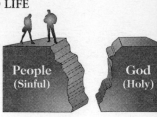

The BIBLE says ... For God loved the world so much that He gave His only Son, so that everyone who believes in Him may not die but have eternal life. John 3:16

2. REALIZE OUR PROBLEM—SEPARATION FROM GOD

People choose to disobey God and go their own way. This results in separation from God.

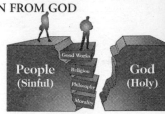

The BIBLE says ... Everyone has sinned and is far away from God's saving presence. Romans 3:23

3. RESPOND TO GOD'S REMEDY—THE CROSS OF CHRIST

God sent His Son to bridge the gap. Christ did this by paying the penalty of our sins when He died on the cross and rose from the grave.

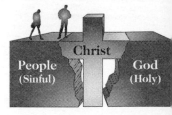

The BIBLE says ... But God has shown us how much He loves us—it was while we were still sinners that Christ died for us! Romans 5:8

4. RECEIVE GOD'S SON—LORD AND SAVIOR

You cross the bridge into God's family when you ask Christ to come into your life.

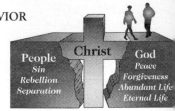

The BIBLE says ... Some, however, did receive Him and believed in Him; so He gave them the right to become God's children. John 1:12

THE INVITATION IS TO:
REPENT (turn from your sins), ASK for God's forgiveness, and by faith RECEIVE Jesus Christ into your heart and life and follow Him in obedience as your Lord and Savior.

PRAYER OF COMMITMENT
"Dear Lord Jesus, I know that I am a sinner, and I ask for Your forgiveness. I believe You died for my sins and rose from the dead. I turn from my sins and invite You to come into my heart and life. I want to trust and follow You as my Lord and Savior. In Your Name, Amen."

If you are committing your life to Christ, please let us know!

Billy Graham Evangelistic Association
1 Billy Graham Parkway, Charlotte, NC 28201-0001
1-877-2GRAHAM (1-877-247-2426)
billygraham.org